HONEST ANSWERS

HONEST ANSWERS

EXPLORING GOD QUESTIONS WITH YOUR TWEEN

JANELLE ALBERTS

AND

INGRID FARO

KREGEL
PUBLICATIONS

To Jay—for suggesting I could.
And to Abby and Grant—for giving me more reason
than ever to need God in my life.
~Janelle

To Janelle—for inviting me on this journey.
~Ingrid

CONTENTS

INTRODUCTION

IT SEEMS LIKE just yesterday that we parents were doing great. Our kids were singing "God is good; God is great" on cue. Their bottom line on Jesus was "He loves me, this I know, for the Bible tells me so," and their habitual last move of the day was an earnest prayer crediting God for pretty much everything.

Christian parenting? On point.

Now, our kids are hitting double-digit ages. As we read Bible stories with them, their questions are taking things up a notch faster than we expected. "If Noah saved two of every animal, why'd he skip dinosaurs?" or, "Wait, why didn't Paul free that slave in the story of Philemon?" or, "Why doesn't God rescue me from having no friends? Our family from divorce? That child from abuse? From poverty? From war?"

Leading up to parenthood, we had vowed to be ready for such a time as this (Esther 4:14). Our parenting plan was to bestow wisdom on our kids without resorting to clichés, so our kids' childlike faith would not stagnate into a childish faith.

Most of us know what that feels like. A lot of us have hit faith forks in the road in college or adulthood. We leaned on our faith, but the underpinning was wobblier than we expected after all those years in church. We committed then and there that that would not be the case for our kids.

Now, at the dawn of our kids detecting the nuances of the Christian faith and looking to us for direction, we parents are decidedly . . . not ready. First of all, who has time to do all that homework? Also, who knows how to avoid oversimplified jargon and still spread the actual gospel in 140 characters or less?

Plus, our kids' curiosity window is closing as quickly as it opened.

Our opportunity to reign as the deliberate, reputable resources that our kids will keep coming to all their livelong days is already on borrowed time, depending on how well we handle the next few years. We can tell by the way our kids are starting to smile a little too wide when they hear our current cobbled-together talking points. They nod politely, but something new is registering behind their eyes: "Ah. I get it. Parents don't know these answers either."

Fortunately, we sophisticated parents of the twenty-first century aren't afraid to hijack a bright idea from the days of yore.

Like the biblical word *dialegomai.*

Dialegomai is a Greek word in the New Testament that means to discuss, dispute, or reason.[1] It is what Paul did in Athens and what Jesus's disciples did on the way to Capernaum. It's sprinkled throughout the New Testament and refers to wrestling with and talking through who God is and what he's all about (Mark 9:34; Acts 17:2; 18:4, 19; 19:8; 24:25; Heb. 12:5).

If one limiting factor of parenthood is that we do not quite do all the homework we mean to do, then the superpower we parents do have is our ability and willingness to *dialegomai.* Our kids need training up in the art of thinking through their faith. That happens by talking it out.

How?

Digging through the pages here is a good start. The Parent Primers are for parents to read on our own, then the Q&As are a way to talk through that with our kids.

We can tell our kids, "Our family is planning to start something new—reading a few short questions and answers each week so we get to know some church stuff that we haven't otherwise talked about directly.

"Also, we will bribe you with *blank.*" (This is optional, of course, but you know, not really.)

Let's attempt to do what we vowed to do back in the day: reinforce our kids' faith foundation at its onset so they'll have less detangling of faith from fiction later on. Let's believe as parents, and as members of the body of Christ, that mastering the art of *dialegomai* is worth the work. Then every time we read these questions with our kids, let's harness our fervor and bombast and commit with all our might to do one thing: keep it short. That way, no kid will secretly pray, "Please get the adults in the room to ditch this idea."

Because ditch it we will. That's how life goes. Our energy will wane. At some point it'll bug the kids when we pull out the questions, and that surprises exactly no one at all. Our best antidote to distractions is to *just start*. Then pick it up again. And a little later, try some more. Whatever morsels we download into our kids will count.

Leave it at that.

Sharing information incrementally, in small bites, is more powerful than we can imagine. We have the backing of parents since the beginning of time who, looking a hard thing in the face, gave their level b-e-s-t, which is spelled different than p-e-r-f-e-c-t-i-o-n for a reason.

One more thing: let's consider praying on our own before running through the questions with our kids. Here's a primer if needed: "Dear Father, these are *your* children, whom I love to my very core. Help me be a good helper to them as they get to know you. Help me believe that you pursue them personally, in ways I don't even know. Help me give them simple information that bends their hearts toward you, rather than any other authority. In Jesus's name, amen."

Let the *dialegomai* begin.

PART ONE

WHAT DOES "THE BIBLE TELLS ME SO" REALLY MEAN?

INTRODUCTION FOR PARENTS

LITTLE KIDS LOVE Bible stories. God holds the whole world in his hands and he loves our kids and our kids can trust him. These are the things our kids know, for the Bible tells them so.

Then kids grow and start noticing all that other stuff the Bible tells them.

"Dragons are real, you know," a young boy once reported to anyone who would listen, holding up a Lego dragon for all of us adults chatting in the room at the time. He'd heard a story in church that week about the dragon from the book of Revelation (Rev. 12:13–17), and he was proceeding as instructed since toddlerhood: if it's in the Bible, it's true.

What do we parents do with that? The Bible *is* true. Yet the Scriptures are ancient literature, and that kind of text asks for a specific discipline from our kids. Namely, our kids must learn how to listen for what Bible writers actually say through allegory, history, or poetry, and resist bending Scripture into a genre they understand as more straightforward.

That is not going to be easy.

One problem with letting the Bible speak for itself is that it includes stories with slavery and killing and "good" characters who turn out to behave deplorably as well as heroically, depending on the page. That's unnerving for young readers just graduating from the sunny Jesus jingles of their younger days.

Plus, the Bible has ancient cultural subtleties that are not obvious to our kids (or most of us adults for that matter), which can tempt our kids to ignore whole parts of Scripture altogether.

Add to all that the mystery of what exactly our kids are holding in their hands. We ask them to memorize Bible verses, but have we helped them understand how reliably those verses have been passed down through the millennia? God divinely inspired the Bible, we know, but by what practical process did these verses come to be in this book?

Maybe that sounds like a lot to lay on a kid at these early junctures. Yet one cautionary tale from our ancestors is this: rich, deeply meaningful Bible stories can become rote, religious incantations if handled incorrectly.

We, the parents of this generation, do not want to do that. In the hopes of avoiding this, we are here to embark on the following short but mighty task list:

1. Help our kids sort through how this ancient Bible came to be in their twenty-first-century hands. We'll sketch out its idiosyncrasies and give a timeline of its basic assembly.
2. Run through the Bible's reputation among today's scholars. We'll outline academic philosopher and ancient historian opinions and clear up conspiracy theories and political innuendos that undermine our kids' high view of Scripture if left unaddressed. We'll gut-check our own parental analysis of the Bible, as well as once and for all purge a lingering, false OT versus NT dichotomy that needs to go.
3. Impart to our kids the nuts and bolts of navigating stories from an ancient writer's point of view.

We parents hereby join together and commit that our answers will not loop back to the *you have the Bible because God gave you the Bible* kinds of answers that served us well when introducing God to our kids. Introductions have been made. Now it's time for getting-to-know. If we ignore the stomach acid that the above task list causes most of us, and if we speak forthrightly with our kids about the Bible, they stand a shot at knowing God just a little bit better.

We parents want desperately for that to happen. We want to empower our kids to lean confidently on the Bible, with abiding faith in its truths, in ways that speak into their current situation. We also want what we cover here to hold them steady as they move forward, so that as they grow and dig into God's Word, the parts that catch them by surprise do not destabilize their faith.

Let's get started.

CHAPTER 1

How the Bible Was Put Together

■ Parent Primer #1: We Don't Have Originals, Yet the Word Is Stronger Than Stone

LET'S START OFF the chapter with this little gem: when it comes to the documents that make up our Bible, we do not have originals, and there are variants in the copies that survived. Most are minor, but there you have it.

This presents a problem that—is it rude to point out?—could have been easily avoided. This is *God's* Word. He parted the Red Sea for Moses and dried up the Jordan for Joshua. Surely he could have delivered to us Scripture originals with no variants.

Yet he didn't.

This can really trip us up as believers. Take Charles Spurgeon, for example. "I was somewhat startled," the preaching giant from the Victorian era wrote when he found a discrepancy in his Bible's version of the gospel of Luke.[1]

We parents are right there with you, Charles. We feel startled when we stumble over reminders that the Bible has not been fed to us like a beatific, bound, enchanted playbook.

However, that didn't stop Spurgeon from being flat-out honest about it. "Spurgeon's most famous break from the King James [Bible] happened in July 1885," wrote Elijah Hixson for the *Journal of the Evangelical Theological Society*. "He began by saying, 'A genuine fragment of inspired Scripture has been dropped by our older translators, and it is far too precious to be lost.'"[2]

We parents can appreciate Spurgeon's nerve to call it like he saw it. We can borrow that nerve when we tell our kids that God insists that rather than idolize Scripture, we must engage with it—not as a thing to be worshiped, but as a gift to be dug into and pondered and examined and prayed over and thought through. Neglect that, and we have a problem on our hands, especially if we promise our kids that the text is above having any quirks.

It isn't.

We get it. God does not ask for utter devotion to a written word. He asks for utter devotion to the *God* of that written word (John 5:39–40).

Yet God does tell us his Word is a light unto our path (Ps. 119:105), which makes it hard to let this go. As parents, we think, "Wouldn't delivering that Word in a dramatic way, say, etched in stone, have made all our jobs a lot easier? God's included?"

Apparently not. Evidently, God is smarter than we are. This is obvious on several fronts, including the fact that he has run through the "etched in stone" scenario before, when he carved out for Moses the Ten Commandments. By the time Moses came down the mountain to present the stones to the awaiting Israelites, they had already given up on Moses, made a gold calf, and said that *that* was the god who had rescued them from slavery in Egypt.

It wasn't.

God does not mistake "etched in stone" as the way to make people believe or even to establish the authority of his Scriptures. He seems to deliberately make the point that we shouldn't either.

Plus, ancient literature just does not play that way. The Bible emerges from ancient times through the same kinds of bumps and bruises faced by other pieces of antiquity, which inserts the Bible smack into history. God acted in physical circumstances among real people. As such, the Bible is rooted in a civilization that developed over time, which can be traced and touched in the same way other ancient civilizations can be traced and touched.

Despite the very earthly development of the Scriptures, however, our kids need to know that the Bible can be counted on with the full assurance of its ultimate author—God.

God said, "So is my word that goes out from my mouth: It . . . will accomplish what I desire and achieve the purpose for which I sent it." What desire and what purpose? "So . . . it yields seed for the sower and bread for the eater" (Isa. 55:10–11). Which is to say, God's confidence in his word does not waver, and with good reason.

"[The Bible] has outlasted kingdoms—many, many kingdoms," said clinical psychologist Jordan Peterson in his series on the psychological influence of the Bible. "It's really interesting that it turns out that a book is more durable than stone, more durable than a castle, more durable than an empire."[3]

Yes. That is interesting. Really, *really* interesting.

HONEST ANSWERS Q&A

We Don't Have Originals, Yet the Word Is Stronger Than Stone

(Parents—remember, these Q&As are an interactive, struc-tured, no-stress way to review with our kids what we just read ourselves. Parents can read this intro paragraph, then kids read the Q&As aloud, or everybody take turns read-ing aloud. Nobody's on the hook to be an expert here; the point is just to talk about it, with it laid out right here at our fingertips.)

We love the Bible. Adore it. We're grateful for it. How-ever, how would you feel if somebody told you that the Bible in your hands has something called "variants"? As in, a word here and there might be different from what the writers first wrote down. Would that freak you out? We hope not, because yes, that is what happened, but no, you needn't freak out about it. Let's talk about why.

1. **Which of the following is a true statement about how we got the Bible?**
   A. It miraculously got passed down from Moses to Peter to Paul and then landed on my nightstand as is.
   B. The Scriptures were compiled over thousands of years. They are extremely well preserved, but we do not have originals, and there are "variants" in the copies that survived.
   C. The apostles made one set of Scriptures at the dawn of time, and all Bibles are copied off that original.
   Answer: B

2. **What are three good reasons we do not need to freak out about the answer to question #1?**
   • God does not ask for utter devotion to a written

word. He asks for utter devotion to the *God* of that written word (John 5:39).

- If God wanted this handled differently, he could have at any time overridden earthly limitations and miraculously preserved Scripture originals. He didn't.
- God wants us to dig into the Bible, and he promises that he will guide us as we study it (2 Tim. 3:16).

3. **What does it mean to find a "variant" in Scripture copies?**
- The church has found old Scripture writings—some were found not long ago in caves—that were *ancient* ancient (some were dated from before Jesus's time, before Cleopatra's time, before Julius Ceasar—like *old* old).
- Church scholars compared these most ancient writings to the Bibles we have today. Where words or phrases were different, Bibles were adjusted and updated.[4]
- For example, a Bible from the twelfth century has a line in John 5 about an angel stirring a pool. That wasn't in more ancient copies of John. Check out John 5:4 in your Bible and you'll see that that line likely has a note by it.[5]

4. **Can we trust the Bible even though it has variants?**
- Yes. Most variants are a word or letter that changes the meaning of the Scriptures ZERO. As in nada. Like not at all.
- Plus, the church has found EXTREMELY old pieces of Scripture and there are VERY few variations. It's crazy just how amazingly it's been preserved, actually.

5. **Wouldn't delivering the Bible in a dramatic way—say, etched in stone—have avoided all this, and wouldn't that have been better?**
- Let's review how things turned out when God *did* once upon a time etch instructions for humans (read Exod. 31:18–32:19; Deut. 9:10–12).
- So, once upon a time, God carved out for Moses the Ten Commandments, but by the time Moses came down the

mountain to present the stones to the awaiting Israelites, they had already given up on Moses, made a gold calf, and said *that* was the god who had rescued them from slavery in Egypt. It wasn't.

- People do not believe in God because proof of him is "etched in stone." People believe because, in relationship with God, he affirms to them that he is real, and through that relationship they discover and believe that he is true. God does not get confused about this. We shouldn't either.

6. **When did we finally have a full copy of the whole Bible with Old and New Testaments?**
   A. Just before Jesus was born.
   B. Just after Jesus's resurrection.
   C. 300 years after Jesus's resurrection.
   Answer: C
   Okay, *that sounds long*, but it was being compiled little by little leading up to that time.

7. **It's hard to drop this idea that God could have preserved Scriptures differently. Does God want the Bible to be just like any other ancient literature? Really?**
   - No. No. No way. The Bible is not just like any other ancient literature.
   - What makes the Bible different is that its story is true, not that it's written with twenty-first-century thought processes.
   - God said his word "yields seed for the sower and bread for the eater" (Isa. 55:10–11). Seeds that are planted, bread that is eaten—it is picture language that can be understood by watching how the people in the Bible lived out the idea in their lives.

8. **Can't we just say, "It says so in the Bible," and let God deal with all this his way? Why do Christians care about all this stuff about Bible reliability?**

Christians care about what God cares about. The Bible is a divinely inspired gift from God, which God gave us through people at specific points in history. If Christians pay attention to those points of history, it'll help us do with God's word what God wants.

———

■ Parent Primer #2: A Sketch of How the Bible Was Assembled

Often by this age, our kids have not only memorized beautiful verses from the Bible but have also learned a few fun incidentals about the Bible—like how many books are in the Bible or what's the order of those books or how fast they can flip to a certain story and whatnot.

That works for bingo games or Bible trivia, but what we cover in the following pages is a boots-on-the-ground style of getting to know the Bible. As in, if a friend at recess catches wind of the fact that our kids go to church and then asks a simple question about the Bible like, "What is it exactly? Where did it come from?" we want to arm our kids with more than, "From God."

We do not want to be a generation of parents to beat this notion unnecessarily hard, but the facts of the matter may leave us no choice. The facts being that the Bible came from God through people's stories and the matter being that our kids will need training on that, because these stories have not been the church's strong suit lately.

"Biblical illiteracy sadly . . . has become worse, not better," notes Asbury Theological Seminary's Ben Witherington. "Even within the church. I mean it's just appalling how bad it really is. Therefore I think you have to start over from scratch and retell the story."[6]

And all the parents reading this just fell over, exhausted.

Start over? From scratch?

Chin up, friends. Any job well done is a process. We parents are not in the middle of nowhere. We are here, together, capable of breaking this down into manageable bits, starting with coaching our kids on how we got the Bible stories in the first place.

The New Testament

Here's a brief rundown on how we got the New Testament.

After Jesus's resurrection, the apostles and other champions of the faith ministered to new believers. As they did, they wrote letters to specific house churches addressing issues happening in that community. Churches kept these letters to be read over and over.

In addition to these letters, several apostles wrote down a summary of Jesus's ministry. These were not necessarily a chronology of Jesus's life; rather, the writers meant to bring out the theology Jesus was illustrating, verbally and through his actions, during his ministry.

These letters and documents were shared among other house churches and eventually became the New Testament.

Sound easy? It was not.

Determining which documents made up our Christian theology took time and was not handled by any one person alone. Believers weighed the documents by asking questions like, Did someone who knew Jesus or one of his twelve apostles write this document? Does this document fit with Hebrew Scripture? Does this document focus on Jesus's redemptive resurrection and bear witness to the Holy Spirit?[7]

Finally, almost three hundred years after Jesus's resurrection, bishop Athanasius of Alexandria posted in his Easter letter a list of twenty-seven letters and documents that churches should be reading regularly. That ended disputes over documents still vying for a spot on the roster and also ended questions of authenticity around documents that had already made the list.[8]

It was official. Hello, New Testament.

The Old Testament

Anytime a back-of-the-bus inquisition regarding our kids' Christianity pops up, there's a good chance our kids will be asked about the "telephone game." In short, how could they believe old, old, *old* stories are anything but a joke, since those stories got their start by word of mouth (aka oral tradition)?

Oral tradition is no joke.

Oral tradition reportedly can be passed down relatively unchanged for thousands and thousands of years.[9] Most importantly, oral tradition is *nothing* like the telephone game.

We parents can illustrate this for our kids through an example. Say a mom at her daughter's thirteenth birthday party whispered,

"The brown dog ran across the road to bark at a rabbit," into her daughter's ear for her to pass down the line to her friends. It would be garbled by the time it came back to the mom, like in the game of telephone.

Let's say instead that the mom told all of those girls, who knew the mom well and knew the daughter, Isabella, very well, this true sentence: "*My* mom, Isabella's grandma, passed away last year, the day before Isabella's birthday, February 7. It was a sad birthday." Then let's say the mom discussed further details with the girls at various times during the party, then happened to be standing next to the girls at pickup time as they told their moms about it and corrected bits that the girls got wrong.

What would the girls get wrong? Isabella's name? Doubtful, since she's their friend who is standing right there and just hosted them for a party. The date? Maybe, although there they were, celebrating at her house in early February. That the grandma died? That it was sad? Doubtful, since they were talking about a real thing here—real circumstances, real people. It was really sad.

That is a better picture of oral tradition than the telephone game, except that actual oral tradition was much, much more strict. Assigned people were trained to pass down stories with extraordinary specificity from each generation to the next.

This was true among lots of cultures, like Bedouins, African and Middle Eastern and ancient Near Eastern tribes, and Native American tribes; preliterate people did and still do handle cultural stories through oral tradition.[10]

Scripture began to be written down around the time of Moses (Exod. 17:14) and included twenty-four Old Testament books by the time Jesus was born. We have since rearranged and broken them into the thirty-nine smaller books of our Old Testament today, though some Bibles include books that were not in the original Hebrew Scriptures.

———

HONEST ANSWERS Q&A

A Sketch of How the Bible Was Assembled

If your friends asked you anything about how the Bible was put together, would you know what to say? Easy questions, like, "Why does my Bible have more books than yours?" or "Why do kids at the Christian school learn Latin? Is that from the Bible?" Or what if friends said something rude about the Bible like, "The way you got those stories is a joke—like the game of telephone." What would you say? Let's run through some background details that might help.

1. **Which of these are original languages of the Bible?**
   A. Old Testament: Hebrew; New Testament: Greek.
   B. Old Testament: Hebrew (mostly, but there's some Aramaic); New Testament: Greek (mostly, but there's some Aramaic).
   C. The whole thing originated in Latin.
   Answer: B
   It's true the Old Testament was Hebrew and the New Testament was Greek. There's a little Aramaic in Daniel and Ezra, because during the Babylonian exile Jewish people began to speak Aramaic, and there's a smattering of it later in the New Testament because it was a common language during Jesus's time. The Latin language was around before Julius Caesar but didn't become integrated into the church until hundreds of years after Jesus died, when a scholar named Jerome translated the Bible into Latin (this is called the Vulgate).[11]

2. **Even before Jesus came on the scene, the Old Testament was translated from Hebrew to Greek. Why?**
   A. Have you read Hebrew? There are no vowels, and it's written right to left instead of left to right.

Everybody was exhausted trying to keep that up so they switched it to Greek.

B. Alexander the Great had taken over huge swaths of land around Egypt just a few centuries before Jesus was born, which made Greek the main language. In order to keep Scriptures alive in a Greek-speaking culture, the Hebrews translated their Scriptures from Hebrew to Greek (called the Septuagint).[12]

C. Everybody had a real good feeling that Jesus was on his way, so they started getting the Old Testament ready to be written in Jesus's language.

Answer: B

It's true that the Hebrew language has no vowels and is written right to left, but that's not the reason for translating Hebrew Scriptures to Greek. They did it because Alexander the Great's conquests made Greek the reigning language of the land, which once again put God's Word smack in the middle of actual history.

3. **For a long time, the Old Testament was passed down by word of mouth (called oral tradition). Is oral tradition different from the telephone game?**

A. No. It's the same, obviously.

B. Yes, oral tradition is different from the game of telephone because oral tradition had a procedure in place to help keep the stories intact. Also, stories and events passed down through oral tradition were not arbitrary goofy lines meant to trip people up like in the telephone game.

Answer: B

This example might help. Say a mom at her daughter's thirteenth birthday party whispered, "The brown dog ran across the road to bark at a rabbit," into her daughter's ear for her to pass down the line to her friends. It would be garbled by the time it came back to the mom—that's the game of telephone.

Let's say instead that the mom told all of those girls, who

knew the mom well and knew the daughter, Isabella, very well, this true sentence: "*My* mom, Isabella's grandma, passed away last year, the day before Isabella's birthday, February 7. It was a sad birthday." Then let's say the mom discussed further details with the girls at various times during the party, then happened to be standing next to the girls at pickup time as they told their moms about it and corrected bits that the girls got wrong.

What would the girls get wrong? Isabella's name? Doubtful, since she's their friend who is standing right there and just hosted them for a party. The date? Maybe, although there they were, celebrating at her house in early February. That the grandma died? That it was sad? Doubtful, since they were talking about a real thing here—real circumstances, real people. It was really sad.

That is a better picture of oral tradition than the game of telephone, except that actual oral tradition had much, much stricter rules, with assigned people trained to pass down stories with extraordinary care to each generation after the next.

4. Why do some Bibles have extra Old Testament books?

Those are Bibles with extra stories about Jewish history (like Hanukkah). They're called the Apocrypha or deutero-canon, depending on who you ask. Scholars largely agree that they were not part of the original Old Testament.

Jerome, the scholar who translated the Bible into Latin (the Vulgate), said that the Jews never used those stories as Scripture and that they had been added as extra chapters to the Bible back when folks translated Hebrew Scripture into Greek (the Septuagint). Augustine, another scholar we'll talk about a lot, agreed that the chapters were not part of original Scriptures but said they tell us important stuff about the history of Israel.[13]

5. How was the New Testament put together?

A. After Jesus's resurrection, the apostles and other champions of the faith ministered to new believers and then wrote letters to them and to their house churches to encourage them. Several apostles also wrote down summaries of Jesus's ministry. Churches kept these letters and read them aloud over and over.

B. The apostles divvied up the writing chores among themselves, hired a bunch of scribes to jot down everything they said, and banged out the entire New Testament while in the upper room where Jesus came to show them his nail-scarred hands and feet.

Answer: A

6. **True or False: The authors of the Bible didn't even write their own stuff. Scribes did.**

Answer: Mostly true!

But believers can't let that bug us. Just because they didn't physically write it doesn't mean it isn't what they said. Prophets, teachers, kings—they all had scribes (trained professionals) to write as they spoke.

7. **True or False: Compiling the New Testament was straightforward, and since this whole thing was inspired by God, let's call it like it was—pretty much piece-of-cake easy.**

Answer: False!

Scripture *was* inspired by God (meaning: it was written by God's knowing and doing), but remember that God works in history through real people. Keeping these documents safe during the early years of Christianity, when one Roman ruler after another was trying to snuff out[14] Christians by burning, bludgeoning, and other gruesome torture was not *easy*.

8. **In the face of so much danger, why would Christians write the New Testament in this way?**

Because they were telling the truth.

CHAPTER 2

The Bible's Reputation Among Scholars . . . and Us

■ Parent Primer #1: The Bible's Reputation with Scholars

SO WE'VE ESTABLISHED that the Bible was put together in such a way that we have a pretty accurate version of what was originally written, but did what was written actually happen?

UNC Professor of Religious Studies Bart Ehrman has reinforced the intellectual verve of Scriptures by noting that Jesus was the most documented Jewish person living in Palestine in the entire first century—by a landslide.[1] But Ehrman also makes the point that the real question is whether we can trust those sources as historically reliable "once their biased chaff is separated from the historical kernel."

Erhman concludes (despite being agnostic and atheistic himself) that yes, we can.

"Historians have devised ways of doing just that," he says, thanks to the astounding number of corroborating historical sources written in Jesus's native language and drafted near the time when Jesus lived. Ehrman says one may align with "post-modern cultural despisers of established religions (or not). But surely the best way to promote any such agenda is not to deny what virtually every sane

historian on the planet" concludes, which is that Jesus was a historical figure.[2]

Scholars also say the Bible itself is rich with meaning and not a
mere moral handbook.

"I don't think a rational moral system is capable of character-
izing the messiness of human existence," says Harvard Professor
of Philosophy Sean Kelly, which is why he finds the Bible intrigu-
ing compared to other worldviews and philosophies. "The Bible . . .
requires a recognition that you can't do it all on your own. . . . Yes,
there's suffering. Yes, it doesn't make sense. And yet, somehow, we're
supposed to be here . . . and we're cared for."[3]

That kind of commitment to honest evaluation of the Bible is a terrific thing for us to tell our kids about. Hearing that the narrative of
the Bible resonates like that even in secular circles can reinforce our
kids' confidence in the Bible when some of the Bible's details throw
them off a bit. Plus, it can help them resist the current culture of iden-
tity politics, which demonizes anybody not in our personal agree-
with-me crew. If our kids do that, they'll miss unique insight about
Scripture. They'll also miss an opportunity to observe Scripture
speaking for itself into the lives of nonbelievers.

What we've heard about God is true: that he loves the world (John
3:16; 2 Peter 3:9) and persists in making that point in ways that might
surprise even his followers.

Modern scholars also testify to Scripture as championing human
dignity in ways no other worldview's literature ever had.

"I thought I could make sense of my life and the world with
resources out of the philosophy of Aristotle. That didn't do the trick
for me," says former dean of Yale Law School Anthony Kronman.
"There's just too many things that I *do* believe that can't be found
there, and one of them, maybe the most important, is my deep,
deep—my bone-deep belief in the infinite value of the individual.
This is missing in Aristotle."[4]

Kronman continued, "Where does this idea, the infinite precious-
ness of the individual, come from? That's a biblical idea, invention,
discovery—however you wish to characterize it."[5]

Yes, that's exactly how we parents wish our kids to characterize it. Knowing that can embolden our kids to wrestle with Scripture in earnest and can ultimately contribute to bullet proofing their fragile will when it comes to being God's actual, out-loud witnesses to his Word (Acts 1:8).

———————

HONEST ANSWERS Q&A

The Bible's Reputation with Scholars

How easy is it for you to think of Jesus as a real man living at a real time? When you hear about famous ancient people like Julius Caesar, for instance, you know historians have some proof he existed. Here's a thing a lot of folks don't realize: there's similar documentation to validate Jesus was real as well—in fact, lots more than about Julius Caesar, even outside the Bible. Let's talk about that. Actually, let's let some Yale and Harvard and UNC professors talk about that—professors who do not even go to church and still say this great stuff about Jesus and the Bible.

1. **What are some examples of what scholars say about the Bible?**
   - Jesus was the most documented Jewish person in Palestine in the entire first century, and we have more proof of him than anybody else during his time. For details, see the Digging Deeper section "Is There Evidence Outside the Bible for the Historical Jesus?" on page 201.
   - The Bible is more than a moral handbook, and that's an amazing thing because all of life is too hard and complicated for a mere handbook. "Yet . . . we're cared for." —Sean Kelly, professor, Harvard University.[6]
   - We all try to make sense of life, and the Bible's story is a great one to do that for one reason in particular: it underscores a "bone-deep belief" that everybody, *all people*, are valuable. "That's a biblical idea." —Anthony Kronman, Yale Law School.[7]

2. **Which of the following ways should you *not* respond if a friend says the Bible is superstitious gobbledygook (not a scholarly book).**

A. "I pity you." Because it's obvious that the Holy Spirit hasn't touched their hearts.
B. "I agree with you because frankly we barely understand all of this." After all, we're all supposed to be nice and not create waves.
C. "You're not part of our club, so you should zip it."
D. Avoid all of the above.

Answer: D

First of all, no one should worry that they don't understand it all. There's so much to learn all along our faith walks that we Christians will always feel like we don't understand it all. Even though we know some scholars say good things about the Bible, that doesn't mean we should expect that we can quote everything those scholars say. Just knowing something ourselves is a good place to start to grow.

As for kicking people out of our "club" or pitying them, we are not in a club. Also, pity is a tricky disguise for love, but it's not love. We pity people when we think we're better than they are. If we want to measure our growth as Christians, our faith will be less and less about ranking people as better than or less than.

3. **One idea discussed in Christianity is that we will only know "in part" (1 Cor. 13:12). Does all this investigation seem rude, like we're behaving in a demanding way?**

God is not a God of confusion. He wants to be known. Yes, we will only know "in part," but asking questions is the process of getting to know that part.

4. **What do historians consider evidence of real ancient texts?**
A. Seemingly meaningless words.
B. DNA.
C. Fingerprints.

Answer: A

They would love to get DNA or fingerprints, but fat chance

of finding that after centuries and centuries have passed. The next question will tell us more about these "meaningless words."

5. **What do historians mean by "meaningless words"?**
   - Historians love throwaway comments that have basically nothing to do with the matter at hand.
   - For instance, Paul refers to "the Lord's brother" in the New Testament book of Galatians (1:19), which reinforced his message not at all and furthered his point to nowhere.
   - Historians like that because it's a casual mention by a writer who actually knew these people. They call it a "disinterested comment." And it helps them prove that the documents are real and describe real events in history. After all, why would you say your great-aunt Ruth said to say hi in a fake letter to a fake friend? You wouldn't? Neither did people a couple thousand years ago.

6. **Choose from the following to fill in the blank: We have more than _____ fragments that help verify the accuracy of the Bible (Old and New Testaments together).**
   A. 10
   B. 1,000
   C. 10,000
   Answer: C[8]

7. **Choose from the following to fill in the blank: That is _____ than other famous ancient works like Homer or Aristotle.**
   A. A bit less.
   B. A couple more.
   C. *Thousands* more.
   Answer: C
   The famous and most documented ancient Near Eastern literature besides the Bible—the *Iliad*—has fewer than 2,000 fragments. The Bible has more than 10,000.[9]

8. **Why is it good that we have all those fragments? What difference does that make?**

A. It demonstrates the importance people placed on preserving and sharing the Bible. It also gives us many documents to show the accuracy of our modern Bible.

B. It makes no difference at all.

Answer: A

■ Parent Primer #2: Scripture Writers' Reputation with Scholars

When kids hit double-digit ages, schools ramp up the requirements for writing and presenting book reports. That opens up our kids for comments from classmates who become newly aware of historical "whodunit" conspiracy theories or are dipping a toe into political opinions (typically their parents'). Are our kids prepared to deal with "I saw on the world's biggest conspiracies list #6: the Bible writers lied about what happened. Jesus was just a man, not God" kinds of comments?

We parents know it's not good to give credence to silliness, and some of the conspiracy theories around Scripture are just that. However, our kids are advancing past the kiddie stages of faith, and their subsequent high view of Scripture is still under construction. *Childish* faith grown into *childlike* faith actually takes a deliberate cultivation, but that can blow up in our faces if kids ingest rumors that this ancient Bible got into their twenty-first-century hands by way of propagandist lies.

Every generation faces the same basic conspiracy theories around the Bible, namely, that the Scriptures were drafted to push a political agenda, though the specifics of said political agenda vary depending on who's making the accusation.

Take the idea that Jesus was not only a man, but *God* become man. Critics allege that the God-man story line was beefed up in order to compete with that era's Greek myths and drive an agenda.[10]

However, what agenda could the disciples have possibly had? Christians foisted Jesus into divine strata to legitimize what exactly? His speech about practicing what you preach and not being a showboat (Matt. 23:3)? His conversation with the woman at the well when nobody else would talk to her, including his own disciples, who thought it was weird that he was bothering with her in the first place (John 4:27)? His blow-your-top-at-injustice attitude in one chapter (Matt. 21:12) that went out the window in favor of keeping-your-mouth-shut-at-all-costs strategy a few chapters later (Matt. 27:14)?

If early Christians were making Jesus's divinity an add-on that pushed an agenda, they neglected to edit the rest of the New Testament to match.

"Aspects of the Jesus story simply would not have been invented by anyone wanting to make up a new Savior," says UNC Professor of Religious Studies Bart Ehrman. "The messiah was to be a figure of grandeur and power who overthrew the enemy. Anyone who wanted to make up a messiah would make him like that."[11]

Plus, if conspiracy recruits were hoping to position Jesus as something akin to Greek gods, they missed the mark on that too.

"It's not as though the Greek gods never come down to earth . . . but when they do this, something interesting happens," says Harvard Professor of Philosophy Sean Kelly. "The humans, they become something more than human—they're taller and handsomer and they smell better and their locks are curlier. Jesus is the opposite. Jesus comes down in *the* most humble form . . . he's the one who has to suffer. It's exactly opposite."[12]

Jesus's stories do not contribute cleanly to any one political agenda in the history of ever. However, a modern problem confounding this issue is that it's not only conspiracy theorists who try to shove the Bible into a propaganda narrative—Christians have too. One example: Bible verses like Romans 13:1–7 were used to support the South African apartheid.[13] Political leaders pressured people by saying God ordained those who had power. So if you were a subordinate crushed by the system? You were stuck with it.

We, the parents of this generation, do not want to pass that kind of twisted heritage on to our kids. But what strong defense will help kids reject Scripture propagandist theories and also deter them from becoming propagandists themselves? How do we graduate them into critical thinkers with a high view of Scripture?

This may have less to do with a *view* of Scripture than with *slogging through* Scripture. It takes hard work and wrestling and reminding and revisiting and resisting easy answers in order to get to an *honest* view of Scripture, or even an *accurate* view of Scripture, before our kids can develop a high one.

HONEST ANSWERS Q&A

Scripture Writers' Reputation with Scholars

Funny books like Dan Gutman's *Miss Small Is Off the Wall* make conspiracy theories sound fun in second and third grade. Now that your classmates are carrying around much bigger books that take everything more seriously, are you ready to field weird conspiracy questions about your own faith? These odd observations can feel like a gut punch, as if our friends are making fun of God, and that hurts because he means so much to us. We might like to punch back.

But there are some things we can do before it comes to all that. We can start by knowing some facts for ourselves.

1. **What is "propaganda"?**
   Propaganda is when you twist truth because you are hoping to get someone to think what you want them to think instead of them figuring out what they think on their own.

2. **What is one accusation of propaganda that gets lobbed at the Bible?**
   One example[14] is that some people say Jesus was a man and only a man, not God, and the writers of the Bible added all the Jesus-was-God stuff after Jesus's crucifixion in order to glitz up his story. But if that was the case, the disciples neglected to change the rest of Jesus's story to match.

3. **What are some Bible passages that show that Jesus's goal in life was not "glitz" and that the disciples didn't change Jesus's story to make him look better?**
   - Matthew 23:1–7 is a good one. It's Jesus saying the Pharisees do not practice what they preach.

That's not a fast track to having power at that time or a way to fit in with the cool crowd.

- In John 4, Jesus speaks with a woman at a well in the middle of the day even when the social norm at the time was to refrain from this.
- Matthew 21:12 and 27:14 are two good additions because in one Jesus hollers out loud about the injustice of a situation, then in the second one he says nothing about the injustice of a situation. Literally, nothing. Jesus acts according to a situation, not to any stereotypically earthly agenda.

4. **If someone doesn't believe the Jesus-is-God part of the story, why wouldn't they just say, "I don't believe that," instead of saying, "That's a conspiracy and propaganda"?**
   A. Because the church hasn't had a perfect reputation of using the Bible in good ways. So in some cases, people have been right to avoid falling for some things the church has claimed about Jesus or about what the Bible says.
   B. Because people are jerks.
   Answer: A
   There are multiple reasons for this, and yes, certainly people can sometimes just be jerks. However, one reason for people thinking our Bible is built on propaganda is because Christians have, well, used the Bible for propaganda. If we hadn't done that, we would have a better rationale for going with the answer B.

5. **When did the church use the Bible as propaganda?**
   A. When defending people in power during the South African apartheid by using Romans 13:1–7 inappropriately.[15]
   B. During the Civil War when the South used the Bible to defend kidnapping whole families, then tearing them apart and enslaving them.[16]
   C. Both of the above, and we wish these were the only times.
   Answer: C
   The fact that the Bible has been used for propaganda in the

past is one good reason to really know what the Bible is all about. That way, it's harder for people to convince us that the Bible says things it doesn't really say.

6. **What can a kid do to keep people from saying the Bible is propaganda?**

Here's an idea. Consider saying one thing that debunks it from the perspective of Jesus, and saying a second thing that debunks it from the perspective of culture at that time. You can use the Bible verses from question #3 to debunk it Jesus-style. To debunk it culturally, try this:

Back in Jesus's time, Greek gods were talked about all the time because Greek mythology was a big thing during the centuries leading up to Jesus. But those stories are *way* different than the God-and-man story of Jesus.

7. **Although Christians say that Greek myths are not like our Bible, does that really carry any weight with people accusing the Bible of propaganda?**

- Not just Christians say that there are differences.
- Harvard Professor of Philosophy Sean Kelly says it too. He notes that although Greek gods come down to earth, it's not like the Jesus story. "Jesus comes down in the most humble form . . . he's the one who has to suffer," Kelly says. "It's exactly the opposite."[17]
- Even an atheistic, agnostic professor said, "Moreover, aspects of the Jesus story simply would not have been invented by anyone wanting to make up a new Savior. . . . The messiah was to be a figure of grandeur and power who overthrew the enemy. Anyone who wanted to make up a messiah would make him like that."[18]
- So where's the propaganda?

———

■ Parent Primer #3: The Old Testament's Reputation Versus the New Testament's Reputation

Some of us parents have a confession to make. We have been known to accidentally paint the Old Testament God to look a little like King George from the musical *Hamilton*. He warned his rebelling revolutionaries that if they left him, they'd rue the day. If push came to proverbial shove, he said he would annihilate them. Why? To remind them of his power? No. To remind them of something else: his love.[19]

Sound twisted? That was likely Lin-Manuel Miranda's point. Behaviors of all kinds are justified by the idea that they were done out of "love." This fact makes the Old Testament God's justice tricky to bear witness to, without corrupted ideas of "love" and "justice" hijacking a narrative of actual love.

"The narrative that gets told in the Old Testament is . . . a kind of care that God has for you," said Harvard Professor of Philosophy Sean Kelly in his 2016 presentation to the Veritas Forum.[20] "That obliges you to recognize the world as a place that you've got stewardship over . . . to cultivate in yourself the ability to do that kind of stewardship work."

We parents can use this kind of precise language to avoid selling our kids on a Lord who claims to love people but actually just wants to boss everybody around. That's not how the story goes.

Leave it to Jesus to clear it up for us. Jesus explained God and expressed his love and survived satanic attacks by quoting the Word (Matt. 4:4, 7, 10; Luke 4:4, 8, 12). To be more specific, which parts of the Scriptures are especially important according to Jesus?

All of them.

"If you believed Moses, you would believe me, for he wrote about me. But since you do not believe what he wrote, how are you going to believe what I say?" (John 5:46–47).

That stands to reason since, although the ancient writers had unique personalities and writing styles, the main character of the Bible, God, claims primary credit for authoring the whole thing (2 Tim. 3:16; Heb. 1:1). Yet, for some reason, we parents of this generation have been known to attribute words like "care" and "stewardship" to the New Testament and "law, law, law" to the Old Testament.

On the contrary, God evangelized Nebuchadnezzar (Dan. 3:26–29), forgave David (a lot) (2 Sam. 11–12; Ps. 51), soothed Elijah with bread and water and rest when he wanted to quit (1 Kings 19:1–9), and legitimized an otherwise scandalized Tamar with her father-in-law's declaration, "She is more righteous than I" (Gen. 38:26)—which, by the way, landed Tamar and said father-in-law in the lineage of Jesus Christ.

In scene after scene, despite hard circumstances and some weird story lines in the Old Testament, heart still trumped all. "People look at the outward appearance, but the LORD looks at the heart" (1 Sam. 16:7). Mercy was there from page one. So was forgiveness, like God telling Jeremiah out loud, "For I will forgive their wickedness and will remember their sins no more" (Jer. 31:34). From the beginning, the God who personally saves was coming—and was already there the whole time.

Granted, some Old Testament stories are rough and raw and confusing. In other words, the stories look a lot like real life during ancient times.

It is hard to get a grip on stories that are saying something about real life. Yet we want to teach our kids to try, and we can encourage this by setting the Old and New Testaments free from any reputation built on our bad reading habits.

———

The Old Testament's Reputation Versus the New Testament's Reputation

Some of us parents have a confession to make. We have been known to accidentally mess up how God is portrayed in the Old Testament. Those stories can be hard for us to explain. But we are going to try. We do not want you to have a subtle, quietly planted seed from us that the Old Testament God is mean and the New Testament God is nice. That's not how the story goes. He's the same God in both sets of stories. To that end, let's revisit some things about the God of the whole Bible.

1. **Is it true that the Old Testament only talks about God being "mean" and the New Testament only talks about him being "nice"?**
   - It was the Old Testament God who kindly clothed Adam and Eve after the first sin in human history (Gen. 3:21).
   - It was the Old Testament God who forgave David (a lot) (2 Sam. 11–12; Ps. 51).
   - It was the Old Testament God who affectionately offered Elijah bread and rest (instead of scolding Elijah for throwing a pity party when he didn't get his way) (1 Kings 19:1–9).
   - It was the Old Testament God who wrote that Tamar was *good* to stand up for herself in front of her father-in-law, Judah, when nobody else in society would at that time, which we know because Judah said, "She is more righteous than I." And then God made sure Tamar was named in the first lines that listed Jesus's great-great-grandparents and ancestors (Gen. 38:26; Matt. 1:3).
   - There's a lot more about God's kindness in the Old Testament—and, not to bring up bad news,

HONEST ANSWERS Q&A

but it was the *New* Testament where Ananias and Sapphira keeled over dead because they lied (Acts 5:1–11). Lots of these stories throughout the whole Bible need talking out.

- Mercy was there from the beginning (Gen. 3:21; Exod. 34:6).
- That God longed for people's hearts over law (burnt offerings) was there from the *beginning* (1 Sam. 15:22; Ps. 51:16; Isa. 1:11–17).

2. Which Scriptures are the most important to Jesus?
A. Everything in red letters in the New Testament because that's stuff Jesus said and of course Jesus values that most.
B. Everything after people started writing stuff down because no matter what you said about oral tradition, all the Scripture from that time still sounds dodgy.
C. All of it.
Answer: C

3. How do we know that all the Scriptures are important?
Although the ancient writers had unique personalities and writing styles, the main character of the Bible, God, claims primary credit for authoring the whole thing.

4. What are some scriptural examples to verify that God feels that way?
- "All Scripture is God-breathed and is useful for teaching, rebuking, correcting and training in righteousness" (2 Tim. 3:16).
- "If you believed Moses, you would believe me, for he wrote about me. But since you do not believe what he wrote, how are you going to believe what I say?" (John 5:46–47).

5. What is one of the biggest misconceptions about the God of the Old Testament?
That the Old Testament is all law, all the time, when in fact, in scene after scene, despite hard circumstances and some weird

story lines, *heart* still trumped all. Just as in the New Testament, God cared about what's going on *inside* people, not just the behavior demonstrated on the outside. It was the Old Testament where God made the point that "people look at the outward appearance, but the LORD looks at the heart" (1 Sam. 16:7).

CHAPTER 3

Ancient Literature from Scripture Writers' Points of View

■ Parent Primer #1: The Ancient Writers' Goal Is Not Easy and Uncomplicated Story Lines

THE BIBLE ANSWERS what it *wants* to answer, not necessarily what our kids *demand* it to answer. Our crew of modern kids is not going to like that.

Take the Cain and Abel story, for instance. God looked with favor on Abel's offering, but not Cain's. Why? The Lord told Cain he would be accepted if he acted *yatab* (Hebrew word for "rightly" or "well," Gen. 4:7).

Interestingly, the Bible only spends a few lines covering that. What's the rush? Wouldn't God like to round out that *yatab* business and maybe confirm, say, three steps to being our best *yatab* self?

Sure. He's happy to. Just not on that page and not in that story.

Wherein we parents introduce our kids to this formidable educator: ancient literature. If we were brave, we might say something like: "Kids, meet ancient literature. It's here to teach you what it wants you to know, not reflexively respond according to what you want to ask. Its main concern is not your feelings. Its main concern is to do what its author sets it out to do. If you diligently adjust your modern learning style to bend to the way of ancient literature's teaching style, the information you can glean from the Bible is practically endless."

Most of us parents do not say that. Instead, occasionally, and again totally by accident, we parents have been known to play this thing a *whole other way*. We parents generally would like to circle all the Scripture stories back into a pamphlet-size repeating loop of easy application. We would like to squeeze these ancient stories into *plain* and *simple* deployment.

Alas, Scripture will not be played that way. For example:

- It isn't plain to us why the author of the Bible makes a command that we should not lie (Exod. 23:1), only to showcase a few pages later a pivotal character named Rahab, who heroically rescued Israelite spies by lying through her teeth. A lot of times. With great panache (Josh. 2).
- It isn't plain to us why Jesus always and in every circumstance says to "follow me," yet when a man healed from demon possession tried to literally do just that, Jesus said no and told him to go home instead (Luke 8:26–39).
- It isn't plain to us why the author of Deuteronomy tells the Israelites to steer clear of marrying Moabites, only to then write a major story line featuring an Israelite *marrying a Moabite* like it's a great idea. Plus, the author portrays the Moabite woman as worthy of our utmost respect, and ends the story by calling her out as Jesus's great-great (great-great) grandma (which, *why point that out?*). We get that it's deliberate, but can we just say that that is not a plain and simple way to round out Deuteronomy's dictate to steer clear of the Moabites, much less marry them, much less save the world with one of them listed on the family tree (Ruth 4:13–15; Matt. 1:1–6)?

We parents are tempted to package the Bible in ways that run easy, uncomplicated lines from times of yore to times of today. That derails fast because the Bible doesn't even run easy, uncomplicated lines from the book of Deuteronomy to the book of Ruth.

Easy and *uncomplicated* do not seem to be what the Bible is determined to dispense. Insisting a complicated thing is simple does not make it simple. It makes its rich parts harder to reach.

What's a parent to do with that?

Believe that *real* is better than easy and uncomplicated. It's messier, but we parents can forgive ourselves for our jangled nerves on the matter. Remember that even spiritual giants like Charles Spurgeon could get rattled by all this blessed truth and still trust in his Word.

God promises us parents that the Bible is God's story, messy though that is, meeting our kids, messy though they are. God makes himself known to them in ways that are palpable and concrete yet also require faith, because his presence cannot be bottled or touched.

Yet God can be recognized.

Put another way, what happened to Rahab and the healed man and Ruth and others? They recognized the same God. They came to believe.

We so badly want that for our kids too.

———————

The Ancient Writers' Goal Is Not Easy and Uncomplicated Story Lines

We know that God wants us to get to know him through his Word, and yet the way that Word is written can be confusing to us. If God wanted us to know him, wouldn't it have been better for him to write the Bible in a way that we can easily decode, using our twenty-first-century reading style?

Well, he didn't.

Since that is not the way God handled Scripture, it's on us to work on understanding his writing. We can do that easier if we set expectations for ourselves. Let's talk about a few of those.

1. **Which of these is a good way to describe how ancient literature speaks to us as twenty-first-century readers?**

   A. Ancient literature uses different styles of writing (poetry, allegory, history) that do not read like news reports or textbooks today.

   B. Ancient literature can leave off whole chunks of a story that we think would have been interesting.

   C. Ancient literature tells us what it *wants* to tell us, not necessarily what we *ask* it to tell us.

   D. All of the above.

   Answer: D

2. **What's an example of the Bible leaving off a chunk of a story that the reader might have liked to have included?**

   A good example is the Cain and Abel story. God looked with favor on Abel's offering but not Cain's. It would be nice to know why. We would like to offer an Abel offering and steer clear of a Cain offering!

More information on how exactly, precisely to do that in our twenty-first-century life now would be handy. Why not give us three steps to do and three things to avoid?

3. **If we are confused about one part of the Bible, what should we do?**
   A. Stop reading. If something is hard, it's not worth it, so forget it.
   B. Keep reading. What is confusing in one part of the Word can be clarified in another section of the Bible.
   C. Assume everybody knows the answer and it's not right to feel confused by *God's holy Word*, therefore zip it. Don't tell anybody and carry on.

   Answer: B

   Also ask questions. Ask parents, ask friends who have some Bible training, and look up answers in a study Bible. God's Word is to be dug into. God can handle your questions . . . in fact, the Bible makes it clear that he invites your questions (James 1:5).

4. **True or False: If you're confused by the Bible and you just keep reading, the answers will be obvious in just a few pages.**
   Answer: True *and* false.

   Believers are careful about words like *obvious*. Sometimes the Bible is obvious. Sometimes not. The key is not to get all flustered and derailed about an answer that is hard or confusing. The goal of Scripture is for us to get to know God. Remember? So the point is to keep looking for God even if you're a little confused at the moment.

5. **What are some examples of the Bible being *true*, but also *not obvious*?**
   - The Bible says don't lie, then features Bible hero Rahab saving the day by lying through her teeth (Exod. 23:1; Josh. 2).
   - The Bible says don't marry a Moabite, then features Bible hero Boaz *marrying a Moabite*. Then the story says that's

awesome. Then the story presents the Moabite as a woman worthy of our utmost respect, plus it points her out again later by featuring her in the lineage of Jesus (Ruth 4:13–15; Matt. 1:1–6).

6. Those examples reveal which of the following?
   A. That God contradicts himself, so we can't trust that writing.
   B. That the Bible is about real life and relationships, not a list of rules. At the very least, these examples reveal God's character through real-life relationships, rather than easy, uncomplicated story lines.
   C. That all those scribes must have written something down wrong.

   Answer: B

   Life is complicated. We Christians stand on the Word of God, not the easy platitude of religion. That means the Bible isn't a bunch of easy, uncomplicated story lines that fit on a sunny sticky note. There is no way we could learn about our complicated lives that way. And, for the record, we're grateful that God isn't too simple for life's twists and turns.

———————

■ Parent Primer #2: Ancient Literature's Conflicting Stories and Contrasting Culture

When Palm Sunday rolls around and we parents read with our kids about Jesus coming to town, does the story feature palm branches on the road, or just cloaks? And was it a donkey or a donkey plus a colt? Also, had Jesus gotten that animal, or did he have one of his crew fetch it?

The answer? Depends which gospel story we parents read. They're different. You can check it out for yourself in Matthew 21:1–11; Mark 11:1–11; Luke 19:28–44; and John 12:12–19.

Welcome to reading eyewitness accounts from a long, long, *long* time ago. "As an historian . . . you put the data on the table," says New Testament scholar N. T. Wright. "The question, as with natural science actually, is how do you get into the data, how you make sense of it?"[1]

Turns out that getting into the "data" of the God-breathed Bible does not mean God breathed it into something outside the material constructs of ancient literature (2 Tim. 3:16–17). Stories that are meant to tell the same event but from a different point of view will look, well, *different*.

Essentially, reading the Bible, as with any ancient literature, demands discussion, direction, reading all the pages, and looking for consistencies and connections between the various story lines and the turns of events and the character of God across the *whole thing*.

That works well for a God who is building a relationship, precept upon precept, and who seems rather optimistic that that way of our kids getting to know him is actually going to work. For parents of twenty-first-century kids? This is not an easy sell. Then again, why would it be? Real life is paradoxical and contradictory and not easy. The Bible handles that reality rather honestly, if not comfortably.

"The biblical author is an ancient Israelite . . . although it is God ultimately," said John Walton, professor of Old Testament studies at Wheaton College. "My approach to any passage is, 'What is it that this author and his audience understood?' Because that's how God chose to work."[2]

However, as we noted earlier, this is not to say that all of Scripture is just another rendition of general ancient literature. Bible writers differentiated themselves from other cultures at the time in dramatic ways.

Take our creation story, for example, in which the material, created world was considered to be, well, something very *good*. "God saw all that he had made, and it was very good" (Gen. 1:31). As noted by Nancey Murphy, professor of Christian philosophy at Fuller Theological Seminary, that's different from other stories of the time.[3]

Compare the Bible's story to the Babylonian creation story about Marduk, for instance, where his best-god-of-all status is secured after he thwarts evil coming at him in the form of a dragon, which he cuts to pieces, and that makes the world.

Because that was a story about the earth being created, as Murphy describes, through a "battle between gods, we know to look in our creation story to say, 'Wait a minute, is violence intrinsic to the very creation of our universe?' And we find it very clearly written that no, it's not."[4] In other words, having our young readers look at other pertinent literature can illumine points about our creation story's uniqueness in comparison, which is good intellectual practice for any of us.

It's important that we train our kids to detect what genre the author is writing in, since what may be obvious in the original language is not necessarily obvious in our kids' Bible translations.

"For example, the phrase that God created things and it was formless and void . . . in Hebrew is '*tohuw bohuw*' (pronounced toe-hoo waboe-hoo)," said Asbury Theological Seminary's Ben Witherington. "In other words it has rhythm, it has rhyme . . . so this is poetic prose if not just a straight up poem, using figurative language."

Witherington went on, "What I say about the Bible is, interpret figurative language figuratively, interpret literal language literally."[5]

So, digging into Scripture from the writer's point of view is a multifactorial endeavor that takes investigation and conversation. The technical term for this, *exegesis*, means essentially getting a grip on what the writer is trying to say, from the writer's point of view.[6]

That might sound like a bit of a free-for-all, but it's not. The Bible is concrete enough to resist scholars coming along and rewriting the author's original intent.

One example of this is a questionable consonant added to a Bible character's name right around the thirteenth century, which switched the name of a woman (Junia), whom Paul called a fellow apostle, into a man's name (Junias) that landed in a printed version of the NIV Bible.[7] However, that didn't agree with the most ancient Scripture fragments the church has. In 2011, scholars published new editions of the NIV. Based on the oldest Scripture fragments, scholars updated Junia back to its earliest rendering and addressed other issues as well, such as fixing verses that had inaccurately used the exclusive term "men" when the original Greek noun, *anthropos*, included women as well, like our word "humanity."

Thanks to all of that checking and double-checking that our scholars do, we parents can sell our kids on the fact that, compared to other literary fragments of its time, the Bible is a stable, astoundingly well-preserved work of antiquity—because it is.

But buying off on its legitimacy is not the same as believing its God. For that, things will have to get personal. That may not happen right away. That makes us all vulnerable—especially God, who positions himself to be accepted or rejected by the very people he created and died for and for whom he wrote his Word.

Working out that tension makes our kids a lot like the Bible characters. They may have personal questions (join the club) about their journey and about the Bible, but they will have to chalk that up to something other than it being an unreliable book. It is reliable, and takes us on a journey that is revealing, enlightening, exciting, painful, and healing.

The truth often is.

HONEST ANSWERS Q&A

Ancient Literature's Conflicting Stories and Contrasting Culture

We get it that reading ancient Scripture will not be as straightforward as those of us in the twenty-first century would like. But once we hear experts break down a story or two, some of this stuff is not as complicated as we might think. That's what we'll talk about today.

1. **True or False: Reading Scripture is the same as reading any ancient literature.**
   Answer: True *and* false.
   True: The Bible uses the same building blocks as ancient literature.
   False: Bible writers differentiate themselves from the ancient literature of other cultures in dramatic ways.

2. **What's an example of our Scriptures presenting dramatically different stories than other ancient literature?**
   - Most cultures have a story of creation. One of those is a story about a mythical god called Marduk who had to kill a dragon and then chop it up to make the earth. Pretty violent, right?
   - But our creation story starts with God gently speaking and breathing into the dark void. Definitely different. So, when people from Bible times were hearing the Marduk story versus our creation story, they knew that the Bible's creation account was talking about a very different God than that of a rather violent Marduk story.

3. **What would ancient people have noticed as important differences in the creation stories?**

62 Honest Answers

- The Bible's creation story is not chop-it-up violent.
- The Bible features a God who made clothes for the very beings who'd just betrayed him.
- The Bible includes a "good news is coming" element when God told the serpent that his days were numbered by an off-spring of the woman, who was coming to crush the serpent's head (Gen. 3:15).

4. **Ancient literature is written in lots of different styles: allegory, history, and poetry, to name a few. What is an example of one of these styles?**

In Genesis 1:2 the earth is formless and empty or, in Hebrew, *'tohuw bohuw'* (pronounced toe-hoo waboe-hoo). See how the middle and ending sound in one word echoes the middle and ending sound in the next word?

Try saying that now. Toe-hoo waboe-hoo.

That's a rhythm called assonance. It's used in Hebrew poetry.

Remember that we talked about how the Scriptures were passed down by oral tradition at first? Making parts of the story have rhythm like this made it easier for the first people who heard it to then repeat it and remember it and pass it down over the generations.

Just as we would read poetry differently than a legal contract, we need to be aware of different types of writings, or genres, in the Bible. There are at least six major ones. For more information about the different types of writing, go to the Digging Deeper section "What Are the Main Genres in the Bible?" on page 202.

5. **When we do the work it takes to read our Scripture from the *writer's* viewpoint, what is that called?**
   A. Annoying.
   B. Fancy.
   C. Exegesis.
   Answer: C

Reading Scripture from the writer's point of view is just getting a grip on what the writer is trying to say. The official name for that is *exegesis*. We're not getting fancy; we're just digging into God's Word.

PART TWO

WHAT IS PRAYER MEANT TO *DO*?

INTRODUCTION FOR PARENTS

ONCE UPON A time, a third-grade big sister decided to pray and pray for her kindergartener brother. She was asking God that her little brother win a prize in an upcoming class raffle. Big sister had won the prize back when *she* was in kindergarten, during a reading contest that culminated with one grand prize name drawn out of a hat. Big sister was so heartened by her win back in the day that she thanked God then with all her heart and these years later she longed for the same joy for her little brother.

Alas, little brother's name was not picked from the hat.

Big sister was crushed.

Mom hoped to help the situation by telling big sister that little brother was okay. Just fine, even! After all, that raffle did not change what mattered most, which is that God loved him.

Big sister looked at mom, gutted, and asked, "*This* is what God's love feels like?"

Nobody likes feeling burned.

Raffle losses can look like trivial matters to us, the big people in the room. And they are. But *trivial* is where God starts to separate the proverbial wheat from the chaff about himself for our kids. God showing himself in the little things is what tells our kids how to cling to God in the big things.

And God *is* showing himself to our kids through prayer. Our kids just need our help interpreting how God is showing up. That would be no problem, except who exactly knows how to do that?

Most of us parents top out at the close-your-eyes-and-bow-your-head or the start-it-off-with-gratitude basics of prayer. Kids are happy to pray like God has all the power it takes to do exceedingly abundantly more than . . . well, just *more*, since churchgoing kids are taught from toddlerhood that there are no limits on God (Eph. 3:18–20).

After some time, we begin to put brackets on our kids' prayers.

Like the idea that they should pray in alignment with God's will, for instance. Prayer is where that sort of thing is meant to be grappled with, yet how can that happen when kids lack a certain confidence in the whole system?

Kids who want to save face or feelings or avoid future disappointment proceed thusly: by downgrading their prayers and playing it safe with Scripture-quoting mantras that calm their nerves or before-bed check ins, like a relative who doesn't want to lose touch.

That's sad.

Prayer was meant for more than that. Prayer was meant to be a conduit to our kids' Creator, our kids' Savior, who engages and intervenes and empowers and *interacts* relationally. Prayer promises to open our kids' eyes to God's will and to tactics that thwart Satan's lies, and to deliver them into a "shelter from the wind" (Isa. 32:2) in ways precise and personal to them.

This is especially true as kids age up from raffle losses to prayers with more gravitas, like asking for a break from physical pain or illness or just one friend to stave off loneliness at lunch or just one more chance that mom and dad might not break up after all.

No, prayer is not to be downgraded.

To help avoid that happening with our kids, we will tackle this short but mighty task list:

1. Outline for our kids that praying in earnest requires praying unedited. We'll assemble the basics of what that means in terms of how to pray and what a good long-term prayer life looks like.
2. Make a case for sticking with prayer even when circumstances tell our kids not to. We'll discuss how to process the hurt and pain of life, and review one particularly fundamental truth about God—that he is real.
3. Confess (and warn) that believers are oddly not great at sticking with God. We'll illustrate how believers of yore ditched God

and how God responded to that issue and what that means for our kids. We'll also reinforce the facts that prayer is more an engagement than a destination and that a key to its success is this: God shows up.

We parents hereby commit that our answers will not loop back to the *just give it to God in prayer* kinds of answers that served us well when our kids were little. They've given it to God. Now it's time to break down for them what comes next. If we parents disregard our knees knocking at the thought of facing that intense to-do list above and proceed to attack this topic one small step at a time, our kids might stand a shot at knowing God just a little bit better.

Let's get started.

CHAPTER 4

Outlining Unedited Prayer

■ Parent Primer #1: How to Pray

LET'S START OFF the chapter with three words on how to pray: practice praying unedited.

In her 2014 City to City lecture, Kathy Keller, cofounder of Redeemer Presbyterian Church in New York City, tells an audience to resist over-spiritualizing prayer. "Think about this for a minute because it's really critical. God wants us to bring our hearts to him *unedited*," she says.[1]

The problem (if we can call it that) with prayer compared to, say, teaching our kids details about the Bible or church history or other more factual aspects to their faith, is that prayer is so utterly intimate. It's extraordinarily personal. Our kids likely have interactions with God that we do not even know about. Their experiences of God probably exceed their ability to talk about what is happening between them and God at any given time.[2]

Therefore, it's on us parents to set the stage for them—that prayer is a chance to sort out their relationship with God as much as it is asking for stuff. A great way to start is: read God's Word, think on it, and then pray that back to God.[3] After that? "Practice, practice, practice. Trial and error, repetition," says Keller. "Just like riding a bike, you get it wrong a whole lot of times before you get it right."

And there you have it, all of prayer summed up in a few para-
graphs. God, the Creator of the universe, in direct contact with our
kids—that's really, really good stuff.

Except.

Here's a real sticking point about prayer, and this will come out
wrong no matter how we try to phrase it, so let's just blurt it out at
the same time: when it comes to our kids, does God really know what
he's doing?

What we mean to say is, does he? Like, honestly?

Because these are our kids. Yes, we say they are God's kids, and we
thought we meant it, but maybe we need practice, practice, practice
at meaning that because seriously, now we parents are counting on
God to guide and correct our kids directly.

Not to be disrespectful, but does God actually do that? In ways
that are gentle and personal? Doesn't he need our parental advice on
how to handle our kids just so? We parents are nutso for our kids,
and evidently that makes it very difficult for us to resist taking on the
role of God in their lives.

Maybe we should remind each other how bad we are at playing the
role of God in our own lives, much less in our kids' lives, much less
in our kids' prayer lives. Maybe we remind each other that we have a
rather full plate playing the role of *parent* in our kids' prayer lives, so
onward we go with setting up micro habits where we get our kids to
read God's Word, think about it, and pray it back to God—then see if
we can get them to do that again. And again. And at least a few more
times before they graduate from high school.

Maybe we parents can remember how good *God* is at being God
in our kids' lives. He's more than able to meet them at their place
of need, even as their tender struggles grow more jagged with every
maturing year.

The Father genuinely wishes our kids would come to him raw and
unedited in their prayers.

Jesus did. Even when it didn't make him look great.

"Jesus had spent his whole life and actually all eternity before that
leading up to the moment where he was going to save his people with

his substitutionary death, and yet when that moment arrives, he's scared," Keller says (Matt. 26:38–39).[4]

In the garden of Gethsemane, Jesus felt with every cell of his being the crushing weight of what was coming. Yet, Keller notes, he did not pretend the situation called for exaggerated piety: "'Oh dear, I can't admit to that, that would be so wrong . . .' No, he was right out with it: 'Can we get out of this?'"[5]

In order for our kids to get a grip on who they are and who God is, they need to feel free to bring the real version of themselves to the table. That includes the ugliness, the anger, the confusion, and even the disagreement. God wants engagement (Gen. 32:24–28). He could have orchestrated this whole prayer idea to be one big feel-good praise fest aimed right at him, yet he didn't (Heb. 4:16). He would rather be approached by our kids in truth, even if they can't drum up an evident adoration at an ugly moment in time.

So, when circumstances are relentless (which they will be) and cries to God are ugly (which he welcomes), let's encourage our kids to go right on ahead. Pray with candor. Pray bluntly. Pray as though God wants to hear the actual truth of what's going through their hearts and minds.

Pray unedited. God can take it.

HONEST ANSWERS Q&A

How to Pray

Have you ever prayed and prayed over a matter, but things still didn't work out the way you hoped? Were you able to go to God with your disappointment? With your questions? Were you able to talk with God about it at all? Believe it or not, God wants you to have these kinds of conversations with him in prayer. That is, any conversations, all conversations. He would like you to get to know his voice so that he can reassure you, guide you, correct you, and show you his affection in personal, meaningful ways. He wants to be your place to run to.

1. **What are three steps to a good prayer?**
   - Read God's Word.
   - Think about what you read.
   - Talk about that to God. It might not be obvious how to do this. Here's a primer if needed. This is personal and depends on the Bible story at hand, but here's the idea: "Dear God, what is the deal with that character in that story? What is the deal with how you handled that moment that she did that thing? Will you handle me that way? Come for me that way? Help me in that way? I wish you would. I love you. I believe you. I wish I could feel you more, like real-life more, like that character in that story. Can you help me with that? I've been watching for that but maybe I'm missing it. Can you be more obvious so it makes sense to me today like it did for that character on that day? And I'll keep watching. In Jesus's name, amen."

2. **Does one always have to read the Bible before praying?**

No. Not at all. The above are general steps, a bit of a framework to help build a structure and habit around prayer.

Often we are yanked about by prayer "how-tos" that either over-spiritualize prayer based on one or two Bible verses or are so loose and without form that we're left without any actual guidance on how to pray.

Praying is very, very important. Turning our prayers into repeatable formulas is not.

3. **Why is praying so important?**

Our experiences of God often exceed our understanding of God, which is reasonable. However, the more we talk to God, read his Word, think about what the Bible says, and notice things we can learn from Bible characters or have in common with them and their stories, the deeper our relationship becomes with God.

4. **As we get to know God better, how do we build confidence in what we talk about with him?**
   A. You just decide; take a leap of faith.
   B. Practice.
   C. You just pretend until you begin to feel warm fuzzies when you pray—then you know you've graduated.
   Answer: B

   Practice. A leader from a church in New York City put it this way, "Practice, practice, practice. Trial and error, repetition— just like riding a bike, you get it wrong a whole lot of times before you get it right."[6] Practice is not just a discipline; it's communication. The only way to build any relationship is to keep on talking with each other. So keep talking!

5. **What example did Jesus set for us when he prayed in Gethsemane (read Matt. 26:38–39)?**

   That we can really say how we feel in prayer. Jesus's emotions over what was about to happen were excruciating, and he was honest about that. He did not cover that up or pretend to feel brave or put on a good face saying, "'Oh dear, I can't admit to that, that would be so wrong . . .' No, he was right out with it: 'Can we get out of this?'"[7]

6. **What about when we're sure God will *not* like what we say or we're just too embarrassed? Too sad? Too mad? Too *something*, and we don't think we should pray about it—what should we do then?**

Pray unedited anyway. Always, always, always, *pray*. God will always be available to you and he's hoping you'll come talk to him no matter what, no matter when, and no matter why.

■ Parent Primer #2: What a Good Prayer Life Looks Like

What does a good prayer life look like? Not just any prayer life, a *good* prayer life. Would anyone be upset to hear that a good prayer life looks like a wrestling match?

Let's flip back a bit in Scripture and revisit one of the weirdest scenes of the Bible, even by Old Testament standards, where a prayerful encounter wrestled Scripture superstar Jacob from jerk status into contender status.

This story line was not the first time Jacob had called on God. He'd actually done that plenty of times. But where we enter this particular story, Jacob was turning a corner from his half-committed relationship with God and appeared determined to have actual intimacy with God.

We can warn our kids that turning a corner and deciding we want to be close to God is not an end unto itself. It's a beginning. And beginnings with God can take a little more time to wrestle through than we expect.

That's a helpful tip for modern kids who are accustomed to being celebrated, basically just for *being*. Which certainly suits God—to God, our kids are worth dying for. They're worth rising for. They're worth crushing the power and dominion of death for. He certainly celebrates their very being.

Yet when our kids engage God through prayer, in even the littlest step toward relationship with God, he likes to help them see a thing through all the way over to . . . well, all the way. That often calls for a little more proverbial sweat equity than our kids expect. Few of us have handled prayer such that we've experienced what *all the way* even looks like.

That night with the angel, Jacob did.

As only ancient Scripture can depict, a wrestling match between an angel of God and Jacob ensued. It went on and on. Finally, after pulling an all-nighter with this wrestling routine, the angel pinged Jacob's hip, and still Jacob clutched at the angel (Gen. 32:22–31).

Why?

For a blessing, as the story goes. What did that mean, a blessing? The angel didn't ask. Instead, the angel's question was this: "What is your name?"

This was a touchy subject because Jacob knew his name meant "supplanter, layer of snares, deceiver." Really, really not something any prayer warrior wants brought up after an all-night angel struggle in which we're longing to take our commitment to God to the next level.

Leave it to Jacob to stick it out though, right there, standing in the light of being seen for who he really was. He *was* a liar. He *had* been a supplanter. He'd deceived people on most of the pages leading up to these lines of this particular story.

Maybe that's how a blessing gets its setup. Before our kids can give the boot to some part of them that needs to go, perhaps an important step is facing that thing in the first place. Especially in light of God bringing it up.

"What is your name?"

"'Jacob,' he answered."

And then, God let Jacob know he was getting a new name. New names in Bible days were a big deal.

"Your name will no longer be Jacob, but Israel"—a word that meant many things including this: "contender."[8]

What was Jacob now? A contender, a fighter with strength, knowing he had God in his corner supporting him, not like an assistant but like a boss who can handle behind-the-scenes parts of the fight that the contender has no jurisdiction over, a boss who likewise roots us on to do what is ours to do.

For a long time, Jacob had not believed that God was in his corner. As a result, he behaved deplorably. More precisely, he behaved like a guy who was on his own. To be fair, his prospects for a support system looked dismal. Jacob's dad liked his brother better. Jacob's mom really loved him, but her scruples were unscrupulous, which landed him in trouble more than once (Gen. 27:5–19).

Jacob had proceeded to behave with conduct so unbecoming that even a sympathetic reader would struggle to see any worth in this guy. But God saw Jacob's worth, even at his worst.

Jacob realized that he was mixing up what was his to do and what was God's to do. It's easy to slip down that rabbit hole when you know yourself to be a liar, as Jacob did, rather than seeing yourself as God does—like a contender. So Jacob lied and manipulated situations, trying in only his own might to handle the needs in his life.

That's not how we have to live.

Yet it is complicated to understand what having our Creator in our corner even looks like. Prayer helps. Prayer connects us to God, helps us see what is God's to do and what is ours to do, and helps us look at a situation from God's vantage point. But as the story of Jacob shows, it might take an unrelenting determination on our part to wrestle it out with God.

It takes real-life trying and testing and proving for our kids, in small but pronounced and personal ways. It took Bible characters pages and chapters and sometimes more than that.

Jacob had known about the greatness of God. However, he had not known until the wrestling-with-the-angel moment that God would do the greatest thing of all.

Stay.

What's a good prayer life look like? A good prayer life looks like our kids are contenders, wrestling out what needs purging and receiving the blessing of assurance that God, under every circumstance, stays.

God is not in a race to close a deal with our kids. God is in a committed relationship to establish a reputation with our kids, one wrestling match at a time.

———

What a Good Prayer Life Looks Like

Okay, this may seem out of the blue, but do you know what a contender is? A contender is a fighter who stands a chance at winning. A contender is willing to keep fighting for a hard thing, even when the situation looks bleak.

Why? Because a contender is not alone.

Back in the Old Testament, a famous man named Jacob was renamed Israel. Why do we care? Because of all the things that new name means, one is "contender."

Christians talk about the name Israel *a lot*. The person named Israel, the people of Israel, the eventual location known as Israel—all of them are a very big part of the Bible story.

That God sees people as contenders is also a very big part of the Bible story. Let that sink in deep.

Do you know that you are a contender in God's eyes? Do you know how to grab that way of seeing yourself and hang on to it? Do you know how to practice it?

One way: pray.

That all sounds nice, but it's weirdly not easy to see ourselves as contenders. It wasn't for Jacob. Jacob's name used to mean *liar*. That's rough. And Jacob lived up to that. He lied and lied.

So how did Jacob go from liar to contender?

1. **Jacob did which of the following in prayer all night long with monumental effect on all of Israel?**
   A. Wrestled.
   B. Meditated.
   C. Levitated.
      Answer: A
      Wrestled. In one of the weirdest scenes in the Bible, even by Old Testament standards, Scripture superstar Jacob was prayerfully transformed from

jerk status into contender status by wrestling all night long with an angel of God.

2. What monumental effect did that have on all of Israel?

It brought that name, Israel, to the Bible scene.

Jacob realized he was getting mixed up about what was his to do and what was God's to do. He no longer wanted to do that. He no longer wanted to strive and try to orchestrate his own happy endings through whatever manipulation and lying was necessary.

That's not how we have to live. Prayer connects us to God, helps us see what is God's to do and what is ours to do, and shows us all of life through God's eyes. But simply having good intentions about prayer isn't always enough. Sometimes intimacy with God takes wrestling a thing out with God.

We can do that as contenders, as fighters who stand a chance at winning because God is in our corner—not like an assistant, but like a boss who can handle parts of the fight that the contender cannot and who likewise roots us on to do what is ours to do.

3. Why did the wrestling match last so long?

A. That's how long a good prayer is supposed to last—all night.

B. Jacob was determined and wouldn't let go of the angel until he blessed him.

Answer: B

Jacob really wanted a blessing, and the angel took that opportunity to remind Jacob of his name (still *liar* at that time). A liar dared to come before God to really talk with God and not give up on the idea of being close with God? Yes. Yes, he did.

Then, the liar gets renamed a contender. But that takes a lot of wrestling, a point we should keep in mind if we approach prayer (and the answers to prayer) in a rush.

Turning a corner into a new closeness with God can take more time to wrestle through than we might expect or want.

But don't stop trying. Keep talking to God and wrestling it out with him.

4. Did God name Jacob "Israel" after the location Israel?

No, it's the other way around. The location Israel in the Bible is named after Jacob. The "tribes of Israel" refers to Jacob's descendants.

5. What might the word *contender* mean for us today?

The same as it meant for Jacob—that we are not alone or hopeless, but we instead are full of possibility and potential.

CHAPTER 5

Sticking with Prayer
Even When Circumstances
Say Not To

■ Parent Primer #1: How to Process Hurt

THERE IS ONE absolute that even a postmodern nothing-is-absolute generation acquiesces to: hurt. We all know when something absolutely hurts.

We parents need to steer clear of selling our kids on a hyped promise that talking with God keeps us from feeling hurt. God's promise, "Do not fear, for I am with you," certainly is as advertised (Isa. 41:10). Our kids need not fear. God *is* with them. However, life still . . . hurts.

Our kids' place in world history is a mash of contradictions. For instance, global data indicates that some things are going great. Several worldwide wish list items are actually coming to fruition at a startlingly fast clip. Literacy rates globally have skyrocketed since the Civil War, after having been consistently "elite only" for all the centuries prior to that. The percentage of people who could *not* read in 1820 (just under 90%) is now basically the percentage of people worldwide that *can* read.[1] Also, the number of people living in poverty worldwide has plummeted by half in the past thirty years, with World Bank Group calling it "the greatest human achievement of our time."[2]

Yet almost nobody knows about it. Nearly 90 percent of partici-
pants in a global survey thought extreme poverty worldwide hadn't
changed or actually got worse. Only 1 percent knew the good news
of its decline.[3]

Despite good data trends, there remains a "stomach-level sadness"
that looms over this postmodern generation, said contemporary
novelist David Foster Wallace.[4] School shootings are an alarming
trend in America,[5] suicide rates are up,[6] and, in fact, a few years after
making his comments on the postmodern generation, David Foster
Wallace committed suicide by hanging himself.[7]

Life still really hurts.

How do we encourage our kids to embrace the high points of
prayer without guilting them into stuffing their heads in the sand
when it comes to their own pain? Although it sounds simple, forth-
right language may be a good start.

In other words, although we know prayer well, do we *explain*
prayer well? To do that, we all probably need to deepen our own
understanding of prayer . . . even if we think we already know a lot.

Meg Jay, an associate professor of education at the University of
Virginia, writes that expanding our knowledge on a topic we already
know well jettisons jargon and slang and forces us to explain what
we mean, which can "promote and sometimes even force, thoughtful
growth and change."[8]

Can we get an amen that there is nothing we parents would like
more than to "promote . . . thoughtful growth" in our kids when it
comes to prayer? If that takes de-churching our lingo, then so be it.

Disavowing his buddies from their churchy lingo is something
Jesus worked on with his disciples, thanks to their complete misun-
derstanding of the way God works through pain. For instance, when
they saw a man who was blind, rather than showing kindness or
compassion, they asked Jesus what the man's family did wrong that
caused this trauma.

Jesus told his crew that they were dead wrong. The blind man's
family hadn't committed some atrocity to cause the man's blindness.
Instead, Jesus told the disciples that they were mistaken to think pain

or injury or loss is always caused by the person in pain. "'Neither this man nor his parents sinned,' said Jesus" (John 9:3).

We can let our kids know that hurt bears witness to the fact that something is broken—our world is broken or a relationship is broken or God's engagement with his creation is broken. But brokenness is not the same as a verdict that the recipient of pain is *wrong*.

All of which means our kids should process their own hurt and pain how, exactly?

This is where non-jargon language is pivotal. We have to find a way to say, "Kids, even when you're buckled over in pain, there is more to you than you know. The world is a broken place and we need your YOUness here. You need your YOUness here, to survive, and, though you maybe can't see it today, to thrive."

There are times in life that will bring our kids face-to-face with the finer points of Jacob's wrestling story. Like the fact that life is so excruciating that in order for us to believe there is any point in carrying on, God had better be behind the scenes doing . . . *something*.

He is.

But, like Jacob: We. Still. Must. Walk. On. Prayer will help our kids know what that means. Prayer can help them break down their next steps into manageable chunks. Prayer will give our kids strength to take that even one very, very, *very* small, fragile next step. Prayer might even help our kids articulate to us how we can encourage them along the way.

The message of our kids' pain may be a mystery, its malice may be beyond their control to shut down, and its complexity may be more than they can disentangle on their own. However, there is *something* our kids can do. Prayer will help them know what that is.

Prayer will also be an unprecedented balm to their broken limbs during every step they take forward.

We parents are here to hug, console, and encourage them to take time to allow God to heal what hurts. It's also on us as parents to believe that prayer actually is able to help our kids know what to do next. Prayer can help them through life in practical ways that empower, edify, and even chastise them, but do not crush them.

How?

Our kids will have to try it and find out.

"This even works psychologically," says clinical psychologist Jordan Peterson. In his lecture series on the psychology of the Bible, Peterson explains that the way to assuage an anxiety-ridden person is to get them to face their distress in small, manageable, voluntary steps. "It turns out that if I force you to accept a challenge . . . that stress will cause you physiological damage. But if you accept it voluntarily . . . completely different physiological systems kick in."[9]

Many of us parents have a tough time imagining that our kids can do what is theirs to do. Honestly, these kids are still little, yes? So what that they are hitting ages in the double digits. We've been double digits for some time now and we're still white-knuckling what is ours to do.

Not the perfect role model for our kids on this one? That's fine. Next up, we'll pluck an example out of history named Corrie ten Boom and borrow from her example.

———————

HONEST ANSWERS Q&A

How to Process Hurt

Can we start by acknowledging something we all know? Hurt really . . . hurts. And, unlike so much in life, we needn't go looking for it—hurt comes for everyone. We can't touch it to wipe it away or shrug it off. Hurt grabs and clutches at us. We all want to avoid pain, and the loving adults around you would like to protect you from hurt, and yet they can't. It's something hard to accept and even harder to explain. However, we are going to try to talk about it anyway.

Hurt presents itself like it's the most powerful thing on earth, and sometimes it is very, very hard to disagree with that. But hurt actually is not the most powerful thing on earth. It's not. Actually, you have something that hurt wants, and that something makes you more powerful than hurt. It won't always feel like it, but you are.

1. **What does hurt want you to believe?**
   A. Hurt wants us to believe in the strength of hurt more than the strength of something else, especially more than the strength of Jesus.
   B. Hurt wants us to believe *only* what's right in front of our faces.
   C. Both of the above.
   Answer: C
   It's hard to believe in the strength of something else when it's hurt that is all up in our faces and so present. Hurt wants us to believe that what's present is all there is.
   However, what's present is not all there is.
   Jesus said, "Don't be afraid; just believe" (Mark 5:36).
   To say that, Jesus *disregarded what was right in front of his face* in that story. Why could he do that?

Because he knew that the present hurt was not the most powerful thing on earth. We do not know all that Jesus knows, but we
do know Jesus, so we can borrow his faith when ours has dwin-
dled because of hurt and fear.

So, hurt wants us to believe hurt more than Jesus. But let's
not do that.

2. **Do Christians ever fall for the lie that hurt is more powerful
   than God?**

   Sometimes, but we do not mean to. It's one thing to say
   something is true. It's something else entirely to act like something is true. Christians may say God's the most powerful thing
   on earth, but our scared, confused shock at the volume of pain
   in the world and in our own lives sometimes has us questioning
   God's power and goodness.

3. **Is this conversation suggesting Christians should ignore how
   much hurt hurts and just slog through the pain anyway?**

   Absolutely not. But when we know how a thing works, we
   can handle it better. So now you know about hurt—that beyond
   its being cruel and painful, hurt wants to be known as the most
   powerful thing on earth. Let's continually consider practical
   ways to refuse to believe that, through prayer.

4. **What good is it to pray if hurt still hurts?**
   A. Prayer helps us break down the message of hurt, come up
      with a plan to survive hurt, and, to whatever degree possible,
      overcome the hurtful situation, one small step at a time.
   B. Prayer invites us to refresh ourselves in the presence of God,
      who will minister to us in ways we cannot even fathom.
   C. Prayer gives us an intimate view of what God's doing about
      the hurt.
   D. Prayer guides what is ours to do, gives us strength to do that
      even one small step at a time, and builds our confidence that
      God is doing what is God's to do.

E. All of the above.

Answer: E

5. **But hurt will still hurt?**

Yes, hurt will still hurt.

6. **Why do we bother taking any steps forward at all?**
   A. Because taking steps forward works. If we voluntarily face our distress in small, manageable steps, our body systems (which God created) kick in to help us.
   B. Because we get extra points for fitting in to that song, "Onward Christian Soldiers."

   Answer: A

   A clinical psychologist who did a lecture series on the psychology of the Bible said, "Individuals are *way* more powerful than they think . . . these archaic [Bible] stories have something to say to you. They say life is uncertain; you'll never know enough . . . everything you stand on is shaky. But, you still have to stand on it. And while you are standing on it . . . improve it. And that's how life goes on."[10]

7. **What are four steps to handling hurt?**
   1. Pray. Keep praying. Stick with it even when hurt hurts.
   2. Rest when needed.
   3. Discover whether there is anything that we can do. Then do that. Even the smallest little step counts.
   4. Observe what God is doing. If it's undetectable, cling to the promise that God is present right now, doing what is his to do. Ask God for personal reassurances of that.

8. **Which is the most reasonable assumption to make when we see someone suffering hurt that we do not understand?**
   A. That person must have done something wrong.
   B. We need more information before any assumptions can be made.

C. Someone in that person's family must have done something
wrong.

Answer: B

Just ask Jesus. When his apostles saw a blind man and made
the mistake of asking Jesus what the man's family did wrong
that caused that trauma, Jesus wasn't having it. "'Neither this
man nor his parents sinned,' said Jesus" (John 9:3).

———————

■ Parent Primer #2: God Is Real

Corrie ten Boom was the first licensed woman watchmaker in Holland in 1922, but she is most known for her work more than a decade later when she began hiding her Jewish neighbors from the Nazis during World War II.

Corrie and her fellow social justice crusaders were divinely provided all that they needed and much more, until the day two Gestapo officers slammed into her home and dragged her and her whole family down to the street and on to absolute hell—a concentration camp for law-breaking dissidents.[11]

Let's pause on that sobering point for a moment of reflection. We hate to see our kids suffer in any way. So, let the record show, if these kinds of larger-than-life heroes send our kids into a bit of a hope-I-don't-have-to-face-what-she-faced kind of stupor, it throws us parents into a practical coma.

However, anyone who reads Corrie ten Boom's book *The Hiding Place* will find something interesting. The book walks through dozens of seemingly trivial details about Corrie's early life, like the fact that she hated housework. Also, her sister was a terrible watchmaking assistant to their father. Switching jobs with each other gave them both joy and direction and purpose and opened up new opportunities for happiness in their home.

It was through these seemingly trivial steps that God built a relationship with Corrie. By the time Corrie's political leaders began behaving unspeakably, God had over and over demonstrated to Corrie one thing: that God is real.

This is what we parents must pass on to our kids. The greatest thing about prayer is not that it is a way to drum up bravery (although sometimes it does) or a way to drum up gratitude (although it can do that too) or a way to drum up our best selves or toughest selves or most productive selves (although prayer's been known to deliver on all of that). The greatest thing about unedited, engaging prayer is that it gives God an opening to illustrate to us in personal ways that he is *real*.

Not to put too fine a point on it, but our kids can recognize that the God Corrie describes in her early prayer life is consistent with the God described in her later years for one reason: God *is* real.

"More than conquerors . . . it was not a wish," Corrie said. "It was a fact." In the concentration camp, Corrie said, "We knew it, we experienced it minute by minute—poor, hated, hungry . . . the observable, external life grew every day more horrible. The other, the life we lived with God, grew daily better, truth upon truth."[12] Corrie learned firsthand, despite living under rule of barbarism, that God was the most real thing on earth.

Corrie did not drum up a faux "consider it pure joy" kind of moment in her pain and suffering (James 1:2–3). Horrible circumstances like Corrie's get a person to the absolute end of their rope, in which case there will be no drumming up; there is only observing what is.

"Reading the Bible now had nothing to do with belief," Corrie said. "It was simply a description of the way things were—of hell and heaven, of how men act and how God acts."[13]

Corrie observed God in ways that will be hard for our kids to digest given all the depravity of war. Yet God will show up in that same way for our kids. That doesn't mean that he'll make everything pain-free. He didn't for Corrie. However, God will present himself in ways that are inordinately personal and yet recognizably consistent at the same time, just as he did for Corrie.

God Is Real

HONEST ANSWERS Q&A

Hurt hurts. Yet, that does not make hurt the boss. Hurt is not the boss of anything at all.

It just feels like it is, sometimes.

In hurt's relentless pursuit to make us think that it is boss, it uses sneaky strategies. One of hurt's most dangerous strategies is to whisper a rumor about God that goes like this: *God is not . . . real.* Hurt plays this one quite cleverly because that is a hard rumor to shake. That's why stories of deep faith are powerful, because they offer touchable counterarguments to the God's-not-real rumor.

It's reasonable to feel a bit of I-hope-I-never-have-to face-what-she-faced kind of upset when hearing a story of faith amid hurt and pain, but let's listen anyway.

Because God *is* real. Just ask Corrie ten Boom, a woman who hid Jews during World War II.

1. What held Corrie steady through hurt?

Knowing that she was safe in God's will, and also knowing that she could do something about the hurt around her.

2. What hurt was happening around Corrie?

The World War II Nazis brutally sent Jewish citizens to concentration camps, which were horrible places where whole groups were forced to work hard labor, fed practically nothing at all, humiliated, tortured, and killed. Corrie and her family hid their Jewish neighbors from the Nazis, until the day two secret police officers slammed into her home and dragged her and her whole family down to a concentration camp too.

3. **Do Christians have a clean, clear direction on how we should respond in truly hard circumstances?**

   Not always.

   For instance, when Corrie asked a pastor to hide a Jewish mom and baby, "color drained from the man's face. He took a step back from me. 'Miss ten Boom! I do hope you're not involved with any of this illegal concealment. . . . It's just not safe! Think of your father!'"

   Corrie did not know her father had heard her talking to the pastor and presenting the tiny Jewish baby to him. Corrie's father took the baby from Corrie and said to the pastor, "You say we could lose our lives for this child. I would consider that the greatest honor that could come to my family."[14]

4. **Corrie saw her situation differently than that pastor did. Both of them thought they were placing themselves within God's will. Who was right?**

   That's a valuable conversation for another day. For now, let's absorb what we can about how God showed himself in real ways to Corrie.

5. **Which of these is the main reason for the kind of faith that Corrie and her family demonstrated?**
   A. Small steps in Corrie's early life told her over and over: God is real.
   B. Corrie and her family's faith is just in some people; they're born with it.
   Answer: A

6. **Believing God for big things comes from having seen him deliver in small, personal things. Let's read about two examples of personal situations that revealed more and more of God to Corrie:**
   - Corrie hated housework. But she felt duty-bound to do it. Meanwhile, her sister hated assisting her father in their

watch repair store. But she felt duty-bound to do it. When they dared switch jobs with each other, the result was such a joy to the whole household that Corrie realized it was not God who'd been making her feel duty-bound to housework. This made her brave to try new things after that.[15]

- During the war, Corrie's sister was hiding a Jewish girl under her floorboards. When the secret police asked directly if the child was there, Corrie's sister said, "Yes," because she thought it a sin to lie. Corrie was mortified by her sister saying yes. The child was taken captive. Later, though, quite unexpectedly, the child was released. This educated Corrie that God asks different things from different people. That makes it hard to sum God up in a package, but Corrie was in a war and was willing to observe God being real, and she left analysis of that theology for another day. Corrie continued to lie daily, her sister did not, and they both saved many lives.[16]

7. **Which of these is a great benefit of prayer?**
   A. It helps us be brave.
   B. It helps us have gratitude.
   C. It helps us behave as our best selves.
   D. It gives God an opening to illustrate to us in personal ways that he is *real.*
   E. All of the above.

   Answer: E

   One of the greatest things about prayer is that it is not only a way to drum up bravery (although sometimes it does) or to drum up gratitude (although it can do that too) or drum up our best or toughest or most productive selves (although prayer's been known to deliver on all of that). It also gives God an opening to illustrate to us in personal ways that he is *real.*

8. **So, Corrie went through all that horror in order to discover that God is real?**

We should not oversimplify an answer to "Why did this happen?" to anyone, much less with something so complicated as war. What we do know is:

- Corrie was in utter agony and discovered decisively even in that situation that hurt is not the strongest thing on earth and also that God is real.
- Corrie still felt hurt—terribly, terribly hurt.
- Also, as Paul wrote in Romans 8:37, she felt that they were "more than conquerors . . . it was not a wish," she said. "It was a fact."[17]
- Even in the concentration camp, "The observable, external life grew every day more horrible. The other, the life we lived with God, grew daily better, truth upon truth."[18]

CHAPTER 6

Picking God and Sticking with Him

■ Parent Primer #1: How to Get Our Priorities Right

As OUR KIDS develop their prayer life, they are about to notice something if they haven't already. Picking God and sticking with God are two very different endeavors.

Back when our kids were filling in Jesus coloring sheets at church, this notion was unfathomable to them. Now older, our kids have seen some things. Recess can be rough. The back of the bus too, since it usually harbors bigger kids looking to spill the beans on who knows what.

No matter how it comes up, our kids will experience a surprising turn of events firsthand: their youthful professed faith will be challenged in some way and they will blow it. They'll choose not to put God first.

Never fear. Parents who have blown it themselves are here. As are Bible heroes from yore who blew it, then one page later blew it again, sometimes in the exact same way. Perpetually letting something else be more important than God is a failure that all Christians share.

Of course our natural instinct is to avoid letting our kids question the integrity of Bible heroes or our own faith. We want our kids to always put God first, and we are tempted to avoid letting them see firsthand examples of people making mistakes. After all, don't we want them to follow good patterns?

However, that doesn't depict real life. Life isn't easy, and people let other things take priority over God every single day. It's like that story most of us have probably heard while sitting through an executive pep talk or sales staff meeting. It goes like this.

Once upon a time, a professor stood before his Ivy League class of high-achieving students, put a glass jar on his podium, and put in it a big rock. He asked his students, "Is it full?"

"No!" his students replied. So the professor poured in pebbles, then sand, then asked again, "Is it full?"

"No!" his students shouted out again. So the professor poured in water until it brimmed over the edge and asked, "Is it full?"

"Yes!" The moral of the story? His overachieving students said, "You can always do more!"

"No," said the professor. "The moral is, put the big rock in first."

It's a nice story. It accurately sets up the dilemma our kids face when it comes to their relationship with God. *Choosing* the big rock of their life isn't the tricky part. Lots of kids choose God. They say so. They mean it. They sing about it and pray about it and then, what to their wondering eyes should appear, but a life jar jammed to the rim with pebbles they let slide in before God.

This recurring God-not-first inclination we humans have is a very important reason for our kids to develop a robust prayer life. As any honest Christian will confess to our kids, it is weirdly tough to stick with our pick for big rock.

To illustrate the point, we can reintroduce our kids to Bible hero Abraham.

A seldom-discussed story line about Father Abraham is that it was hard for Abraham to consistently put God in first as the big rock in his life. For example, Abraham pawned off Sarah, his wife, as his sister to get in good with an ungodly king. Sure, the king might have otherwise killed Abraham, but still. This was not a God-is-my-shield-my-very-great-reward kind of thing to do (Gen. 12:10–20).

Maybe cracks are inevitable in any character and start to show after a long and exhaustingly faithful life. Except it happens already by page ten of the Bible. And later Abraham did it again.

In Abraham's story line, midway between sell-Sarah-like-a-sister offenses, God locked down a covenant with Abraham that addressed this issue.

It was a "berith," an agreement made by passing through pieces of cut-up animal flesh, which was common cultural contract signing in those days. It is not as gross as it sounds. Simply, two people agreed to something, cut animals in half, and the person with less clout walked through the pieces, signifying that if they broke the promise then they too would be cut to pieces.[1]

Actually, it is as gross as it sounds.

Nevertheless, God told Abraham to set up the berith animal pieces. Abraham did so and then he waited. He slept a little, or fell into a stupor of some sort. Cue the music for the walk-through-the-flesh portion of the show, and behold, a dramatic plot twist ensues! A pot/torch/lightning bolt/divine presence appears and passes through the pieces of flesh. In Abraham's place.

To be clear, God himself took the place of weak Abraham and walked between the cut-up animal pieces. God in essence said, "Yes, Abraham, you may promise me, but what trumps all is that I promise you. Afraid that you will revert, digress, break your promise, and instead of me, put other stuff in your life jar first? You will. I know this. And when you do, the cut-to-pieces business is on me. I will take the punishment."

Abraham, meet rock.

This deserves a moment of reflection.

That narrative is unlike any other narrative among any ancient stories. Here is a story that describes the God who is willing to sacrifice himself on behalf of humans rather than the other way around.

What did Abraham do after he received this extraordinary, one-of-a-kind, never-before-seen-in-history kind of covenant?

He pawned off Sarah as his sister. Again (Gen. 20:1–13).

Putting God first is hard. We mean to. We promise we will. Yet the God revealed in Abraham's story line seems to think people are worth it for him to keep his promises to people even when people do not keep their promises to God.

The degree to which our kids grasp this will sway their prayer life now and as long as we all shall live.

HONEST ANSWERS Q&A

How to Get Our Priorities Right

Remember when you used to sing "Jesus Loves Me" at the top of your lungs in the back seat of the car with the windows open? With actual people walking by? Back when you were a kid of uninterrupted adoration and conviction for Christ? You're a great kid, invested in your faith, ready to serve God's kingdom when duty calls, and yet it probably isn't a secret that faith can slide a bit as you grow. Shocking, right? Today, let's check out people who've struggled a little and find out what God has to say about that.

1. **From the following, choose any that really little kids expect a faith walk will look like forever and ever:**
   - Bold.
   - Fearless.
   - Fun.
   - Easy.

2. **From the following, choose any that, as we grow into bigger kids, our faith walk actually starts to feel like:**
   - A little less easy.
   - A little more complicated.
   - A bit conflicting with friends who do not believe the same things.
   - A tiny bit lonely when it seems like we should say something but we don't. Or like we should *not* say something but we do. And we regret it.

3. **Let's discuss something about God here.**
   We've talked about doing what is yours to do, and watching God do what is his to do, but do you know what that means?

It means that when it comes to what we follow—what ideas or behaviors or really anything—we have to follow God first. *First* first.

Sorry if that seems repetitive, but it's important. First is different than one of many. Of course you would not say God is one of many in your life—God's *God*! Here's a story that shows how we can feel that way, but then accidentally just slot God as one of many after all.

Once upon a time, a professor stood before his Ivy League class of high achieving students, put a glass jar on his podium, and put in it a big rock. He asked his students, "Is it full?"

"No!" his students replied. So the professor poured in pebbles, then sand, then asked again, "Is it full?"

"No!" his students shouted out again. So the professor poured in water until it brimmed over the edge and asked, "Is it full?"

"Yes!" The moral of the story? His overachieving students said, "You can always do more!"

"No," said the professor. And he proceeded to fill another jar with water and then tried to put a big rock in that jar. Let's just say things got a little overflowing and messy and wet. The professor then looked up at the class and said, "The moral is, put the big rock in first."

4. **Why can't God just be one of many rocks we put in our jar? Why does the God rock have to be *first*?**

   Because of God's size. He's not the size of "in after you." He's the size of *first*. If he's not in first, he would have to squeeze himself down to a smaller size to fit, and a smaller size of God is . . . not God.

5. **What does God do when we neglect to put him in first?**

   A. Breaks himself into pieces, compensating for the damage *we* cause in our relationship with him, then persists in reestablishing a relationship with us.

B. Breaks up with us.
C. Punishes us with the silent treatment.
    Answer: A
    A good example of this is the story of Abraham. Let's talk about that.

6. **What's a covenant?**
    A promise, but a big one.

7. **What covenant did God make with Abraham?**
    The ancient word is "berith," or an agreement made by passing through pieces of cut-up animal flesh. Meaning if you break the agreement, you'll be broken to pieces like these pieces of animal that we're walking through (yes, gross, but the person promising isn't likely to forget the illustration).
    God told Abraham to set up the berith animal pieces and then God passed through the pieces and *didn't* make Abraham do it. Basically God was telling Abraham that if Abraham messed up, God would take the consequences and be broken to pieces.

8. **Which of the following best represents Abraham's response to this one-of-a-kind covenant?**
A. Abraham jumped for joy.
B. Abraham pawned off Sarah as his sister. Again (Gen. 20:1–13).
C. Abraham praised God.
    Answer: B
    We don't talk about it a lot, but one part of Abraham's story line is that it was hard for him to stick with his pick for big rock (Gen. 12:10–20). After Abraham had pawned off Sarah, his wife, as his sister to get in good with an ungodly king, God locked down a covenant with Abraham that addressed this issue. But even after all that covenant-making with God, Abraham went ahead and pawned off Sarah as his sister again.

9. **Why would God go through all that bother if people just go off and treat his promises like that?**

That's backward. God goes through all that bother *because* people break their promises to him all the time. His point is to be *God* in this relationship—the one who rescues us and cares for us and loves us. He restores us back into relationship with him because he wants to stay in relationship with us in our humanness, even when we neglect to put him first.

10. **The best takeaway points from Abraham's story are:**
   A. Everybody puts stuff in their life jar before God sometimes, so don't worry about it.
   B. Everybody puts stuff in their life jar before God sometimes, so don't be shocked when you do it. But, also, knock it off.
   Answer: B
   We are to do what is ours to do, which is knock it off with the habitual neglecting to put God in our life jar first. And God will do what is his to do, which is cover and compensate for us in ways we cannot. Let's discuss that in our last section.

11. **True or False: God does what is his to do *because* we do what is ours to do.**
   Answer: False. Really, *really* false.
   THAT. IS. FALSE.
   So false we need a whole new word for it.
   Just to review, the answer to that question is: false.
   God does not do what is his to do BECAUSE we do what is ours to do. God does what is his to do because he is God. Let's discuss that in the next section.

───────────

■ Parent Primer #2: God Shows Up

Kids today get a lot of destination-type words thrown at them, as if they should have already arrived at certain states of being, like they should just *have* faith or they should just *be* confident.

What do they have to be confident about? They're kids, barely getting started. That's a lot of pressure to ask them to assume confidence in an untested person (themselves) or an untested system (their faith).

We have to get comfortable with the fact that for prayer to work, God has to show up. Not like a genie in a bottle or like a wish on a star, but like God. Can we parents admit real quietly here, just between us, that counting on God to show up is a rather nerve-wracking endeavor? Not that we don't think God will show up for our kids, because he will. Right?

Yes, yes he will. He stands between our kids and evil itself. Like this:

> Jesus, *knowing all that was going to happen to him*, went out and asked [the soldiers], "Who is it you want?"
> "Jesus of Nazareth," they replied.
> "I am he," Jesus said. (John 18:4–5, emphasis added)

A thousand or so Bible pages after Abraham twice asked his wife to shield him from the bad guys with a lie, Jesus stepped up to shield us all from evil itself with the truth. Raw political power on earth and the dominion of darkness below wanted Jesus to cower.

And Jesus didn't.

"I am he," Jesus said, standing, facing the enemy. As in, "No matter what you are prepared to do about it, I am standing right here between your evil and all of humanity."

And then, Jesus said it again (John 18:5–8).

God shows up. That does not mean all of our earthly suffering ends. Illnesses still recur, families still break up, children are wounded and bruised.

This world is not our kids' home. It boasts of wonder and energy and more that are parts of our true home, but this world also conspires tirelessly to make our kids cower. However, because of the way God showed up in the past and continues to show up now and in the future, there is a particular cross that our kids will never have to bear.

Even when they do not do what is theirs to do, they needn't cower. On behalf of our kids every time they put something above God, or miss the mark even when trying to put God in their life jar first, or outright pursue something instead of God, Jesus has wiped out the debt owed on that. Every single time. Covered. Paid, if they let him.

Behold what manner of love that is. Absolutely, behold it.

God Shows Up

1. **What can we say about Jesus in light of what we learned about Abraham and the berith covenant last time?**

   A thousand or so Bible pages after Abraham asked his wife to shield him from the bad guys with a lie, Jesus stepped up to shield us all from evil itself with the truth. Raw political power on earth and the dominion of darkness below wanted to see Jesus cower.

   And Jesus didn't.

2. **What best summarizes how Jesus stood between evil and us when the soldiers arrived?**

   A. Jesus stood and faced the soldiers, still feeling every feeling any other person would go through. The next steps were going to be very hard for Jesus, but he took them anyway.
   B. Jesus had superhuman strength and nothing could really hurt him, so he could be brave.
   Answer: A
   The Bible tells us this about Jesus's arrest:

   > Jesus, *knowing all that was going to happen to him*, went out and asked [the soldiers], "Who is it you want?"
   > "Jesus of Nazareth," they replied.
   > "I am he," Jesus said. (John 18:4–5, emphasis added)

   Jesus stepped between evil and everybody else. He volunteered himself. *Not* because people do what is theirs to do and this is their reward.

   That's backward.

Jesus did this because he's Jesus. His love is not a reward. His love is . . . *him*.

3. What have we learned we can get from prayer?
   A. Prayer makes us brave.
   B. Prayer helps us feel love.
   C. Prayer gives us insight to whether or not God is real.
   D. All of the above.
   Answer: D
   All of the above, but especially C.

4. For God to demonstrate that he is real, which of the following will God have to do?
   A. Perform miracles in front of our friends and family on demand.
   B. Show up, in personal ways that might be hard for someone outside to understand but that we can recognize.
   C. Make us feel warm fuzzies in our stomach when we pray so we know he's listening.
   Answer: B
   We recognize God in what he did for Abraham and Jacob and even Jesus in the garden. We recognize that God because we have experienced him too. Not exactly the same, but he shows up in relationship with us through the Holy Spirit. It's ongoing and directed from him to us in extraordinarily, affectionately personal ways.

5. This place is earth (doesn't feel like home), not heaven (feels like *home*!), but because of the way God showed up and shows up, there is a particular cross that we never have to bear. What is that?
   A. Every time we put something above God, God still won't break up with us.
   B. Even when we miss the mark when trying to follow God, God does not break up with us.

C. Even if we outright pursue something instead of God, God does not break up with us.

D. All of the above.

Answer: D

Of course this doesn't mean we intentionally dive into sin. That would be treating God's grace as insignificant in our lives when really grace means everything to us. It means that God will always be faithful to us even when we aren't faithful to him. We don't have to carry the burden of our salvation. He already did.

PART THREE

IF GOD MADE THE WORLD, WHAT'S MY SCIENCE TEACHER TALKING ABOUT?

INTRODUCTION FOR PARENTS

EARLY ON, KIDS get the impression that science and religion do not mix.

When kids hear in church that a whale swallowed Jonah or that one guy and a rib and a woman launched the entire human race, they eventually want to know how these stories and science mesh.

We would like to say that church is the best place for our kids to ask science-Bible questions. We would like to say that it is church where our kids can count on getting comprehensive, consistent answers from teachers and parents and church leaders.

Unfortunately, a few of us Christian parents have gotten ourselves into a bind on that matter. Somewhere along the line, we started an unofficial "don't ask, don't tell" policy around the issue of science and the Bible.

That is to say, those of us who don't know too much about science and the Bible don't want our kids to ask too much about science and the Bible because we don't want to tell them that our mastery of the subject goes maybe one or two layers beyond surface conversation and that's about it.

Our attempts to neatly marry God's natural truths (science) to God's written truths (Scripture) in clear, cogent, concise ways regularly turns out to be . . . none of those words. Sometimes we elevate science; sometimes we diminish it. Sometimes we pigeonhole God's Word on the matter with oversimplified answers; sometimes we cast God's Word as mysterious holy lore with over-spiritualized answers.

Why is this so *hard*? God made nature and God made Scripture. Digging deeper into one shouldn't threaten the truth about the other.

However, the Bible says things that do not make this easy on us, like the fact that God created light and *then* the sun. Also, the Bible calls the sky a dome. As in a solid, hard one.[1] Not to mention, the Bible narrators likely believed the earth was flat and the sun circled it rather than the other way around. Making matters worse, our church forefathers called the scientist Copernicus a heretic for pointing out that that's not actually the way God's physical system goes.[2]

We might have fared better had we listened to church forefathers even further back in time, like third-century bishop Augustine of Hippo. He saw this science-versus-faith issue brewing and warned believers not to buy off on the latest science trend du jour nor feel pressured to reject new scientific discoveries without giving them a fair shake. He said, "In such cases, we should not rush in headlong and so firmly take our stand on one side that, if further progress in the search for truth justly undermines our position, we too fall with it."[3] Almost two thousand years later, we Christians still need a little time to practice that one.

Therefore we, the parents of this generation, proceed thusly: we will act and speak like we actually believe the same God wrote it all. God wrote the laws of physics, and he also wrote Genesis. He wrote the algorithm for consciousness as well as the narrative of Revelation, and he does not ever suggest it's all an easy read, so neither should we. However, it is important that our kids believe that all wisdom and all truth originate from the same author, for one reason: because that's true. To help our kids deduce that, we will tackle this short but mighty task list:

1. Declutter for our kids the science versus faith argument. We'll sketch the history of how the conversation got so contentious in the first place and where the situation stands today.
2. Point out that science disagrees on major points even within its own ranks. So does religion. We'll look into how the science side of the street admits they have yet to explain some of the things they have set out to explain. We'll also check how the faith side of the street has yet to land on common consent on some topics as well.

3. Make the case to keep the conversation going, even when it's hard and answers are not presenting in self-evident ways. We'll drive home that our kids should avoid making science the enemy. We'll also enlist our kids to be brave in conversations that feel contentious and teach them that that doesn't mean anyone is doing it wrong; it means that talking a thing out is hard. However, a Christian heart is designed to be the least reflexive, least peevish, least fragile ego in the room, so having a hard conversation is something we should be handling openly, honestly, and with diplomacy.

We parents hereby commit that our answers will have a high view of Scripture, yet we will not resort to reciting verses like ritual incantations that shut down conversation. If we bravely dip a toe into these controversial waters in an effort to follow the Holy Spirit's guidance, our kids stand a shot at knowing God just a little bit better.

CHAPTER 7

Why Science and Faith Fight

■ Parent Primer #1: The History of the Argument

Emily Dickinson once wrote, "Tell all the truth but tell it slant."[1] It's the first line of a poem that encourages truth telling, but in stages, and rather gently.

If only we parents could break down the fight between science and faith with our kids in stages, and rather gently. It's embarrassing to admit how unjustifiably contentious the science-versus-faith conversation has gotten. Science has handled Scripture anything but gently. And faithful believers have not handled the developing truths of science gently either. Meanwhile, we're the adults in the room. Our kids expect us to do better and be better.

Emily Dickinson would not be impressed.

Of course the irony undergirding a science-versus-faith rivalry from a Christian worldview is this: God's the boss of both. God inspired Scripture and God created the material world. Learning the truth about either of them is learning more about their inventor: God.

Take heliocentrism for instance, the model for how our universe works—the sun is center; we (on earth) revolve around the sun. During the second century, Claudius Ptolemy of Alexandria got everybody believing an old Aristotelian idea that the sun revolved around the earth rather than the other way around. That notion held steady until Copernicus decisively made the case that no, it did not.[2] Thank you, Copernicus! However, some religious folks did not like it. Why?

"As Holy Scripture tells us," Martin Luther said, "so did Joshua bid the sun to stand still, and not the earth (Josh. 10:13)."[3] John Calvin said that minds that say otherwise "indeed confess that the devil possess them."[4]

That sounds pretty straightforwardly anti-Copernicus, although theologians have said Luther was never opposed to Copernicus. They say Luther actually said that when Psalm 24:2 writes that the earth was established on the waters, it simply "speaks according to what the eyes see,"[5] and that the writers of the Bible "describe physical phenomena from their own observational standpoint and not in absolute terms."[6]

Alas, that is not the sentiment that stuck. Instead, the seed was sown among religious circles that science was not to be regarded as a complementary study of God's material world. It was to be regarded as a competitor to the textbook of faith, hope, and love—Holy Scripture.

Thankfully, we have made a few strides since then.

"Both Calvin and Luther rejected Copernicus as a heretic in the 16th century," said evangelical preacher R. C. Sproul, discussing science and church history before an audience of churchgoers. "But I don't know anybody in orthodox Christianity today who is pleading we teach geocentrism. Do you?"[7]

No, no we do not. That's the good news. The bad news is it took a few centuries for the church to develop this more charitable attitude, and that was after it had Galileo Galilei locked up for agreeing with Copernicus on the earth-rotates-around-the-sun matter.

Galileo himself tried making the point that "scientific research and the Christian faith were not mutually exclusive, and that study of the natural world would promote understanding and interpretation of Scriptures." But church leaders didn't budge.[8] Not that that changed Galileo's mind. "Legend has it that as Galileo rose from

kneeling before his inquisitors, he murmured, 'e pur, si muove'—
'even so, it does move.'"[9]

More than three hundred years later, the church officially apolo-
gized, but the early shots of science versus faith had been fired.

Despite all of that, however, nothing had worse ramifications on
the relationship between science and faith than the events at the turn
of the nineteenth century.[10] It was during those years that science
began to present in earnest as the bright, shiny source of strength the
public should turn to and trust.

"Steam engines, electricity . . . inoculations . . . anesthetic, and bril-
liant new progress in surgery were medical marvels which preached
irresistibly the gospel of science," says Bernard Ramm in his book
The Christian View of Science and Scripture.[11] How did religious leaders respond?

Not great.

By the late 1800s major denominations were arguing over which
bits of Scripture were to be read as allegorical, historical, or poetic.
Meanwhile, scientific advances were coming at them rapid fire.
Church leaders had been trained on the classics, yet they suddenly
needed proficient, measured responses about the physical world.
Instead, they often punted the conversations altogether by quoting
Scripture as if that ended the conversation.[12]

"People . . . either want to read science out of the Bible or read science into the Bible," says John Walton, professor of Old Testament
studies at Wheaton College. "That's not the way to do it, because
inevitably you end up making the text say things it never meant to
the ancient audience."[13] The science-versus-faith debate continues to
suffer from this fallout.

HONEST ANSWERS Q&A

The History of the Argument

Have you ever wanted to ask a question in a school science class about something you'd heard at church, but you were too embarrassed? Or have you ever wanted to ask something at church that you heard in science class, but you were too embarrassed?

You're not alone. The adults on the case of science and faith have not handled our chores as well as we could have, and as a result, science and faith advocates draw lines in the sand that keep everybody tense when talking about these topics. It's been going on for centuries. Let's get our bearings on where it all started and why.

1. **Why do you think science and faith advocates argue?**
   A. Scientists have made fun of people of faith since the beginning of time.
   B. Scientists want to investigate and measure the material world around them; people of faith want to ensure a degree of reverence so that all glory of that creation goes to God. Thus, they can get on each other's nerves.
   Answer: B

   Do some scientists believe that science is by definition anti-God? Yes. Does that mean we should assume that they speak for *all* scientists? No.

   Not all scientists are anti-God (and not all Christians are anti-science).

2. **Why can Christians keep a wise and steady attitude to new scientific discoveries?**
   A. We are a tiny bit smarter than the rest of the world, so we listen politely but then just assume we know best.

B. We know that exploring God's material world gives us more ways to know God. Why not be encouraged about that?

C. We are kind by nature because we're Christians. So we pat those little scientists on the head when they use big words because it's so cute when they do that.

Answer: B

Even though answers A and C above are written with a funny undertone, we Christians can on occasion and totally accidentally act exactly like that. If we notice each other doing that, let's mention it to each other so we can grow out of that.

3. **Why is a science-versus-faith rivalry ironic, at least from a Christian's point of view?**

Because God is boss of both science and faith. God authored the material world (what we see and touch), and God authored the spiritual world (what we don't physically see and touch). Discoveries in one should inform the other, not get each other so mad.

4. **If God is boss of both the material world (what science studies) and the spiritual world (what faith advocates for), what should we do when genuine conflict comes up between the two?**

- First, don't make it worse by assuming science is our enemy.
- Second, remember that God's Word is true. With that in mind, think about how we read Scripture. "The Bible is very important to me," said John Polkinghorne, an Anglican priest and physicist. "I have to figure out, what am I reading? Am I reading a divinely dictated textbook . . . to save me the trouble of doing science . . . ?"[14] Yes, it's divinely inspired. No, it's not saving us the trouble of doing science.
- Third, don't feel pressured. Don't get bullied into making a snap decision, as if that's a show of loyalty to God. God knows our loyalty. Take time to think, talk with your mom and dad, that sort of thing.

- A bishop from the third century made a good point about all this when he said, "In such cases, we should not rush in headlong and so firmly take our stand on one side that, if further progress in the search for truth justly undermines our position, we too fall with it."[15]

5. **Why is it unwise to simply quote a Scripture that shuts down science claims and therefore ends the conversation?**

Maybe this sounds totally reasonable because Jesus shut down Satan with one-liners in the desert (Matt. 4:1–11).

But our forefathers also did that back in the day and a guy was jailed over saying the earth circles the sun. Our forefathers said his claim was anti-Bible because, "As Holy Scripture tells us, so did Joshua bid the sun to stand still, and not the earth (Josh. 10:13)."[16] That's bad news for lots of reasons, not least of which is that the sun does not circle the earth.

And the church leaders also did that when big innovations were coming to market in the late 1800s. Believers were saying, "Praise God, not science!" but they were still helping themselves to anesthesia before surgery and electricity in their homes and enjoying all of it anyway. Christians did not break down the conversation properly, and therefore it did not help people get to know how using the brain God gave us to innovate matches up with a spiritual walk and responsibilities in God's kingdom.

It's true sometimes that invoking (praying, saying, proclaiming) a Bible verse is the exact right thing to deal with a conversation. But sometimes a conversation requires more dialogue, like Jesus did with Nicodemus (John 3:1–21) and Paul did Sabbath after Sabbath (Acts 17:2). Being a Christian requires thinking about when to do which. That takes practice. God's Word is the most wonderful, indescribable gift to nourish and guide you on these matters. But adults like your parents are also here to help!

6. **How could church leaders have gotten it so wrong when dealing with a scientific claim?**

Just so you know, that same church leader who misused Joshua 10:13 reportedly said that when Psalm 24:2 writes that the earth was established on the waters, it simply "speaks according to what the eyes see."[17] He said the writers of the Bible "describe physical phenomena from their own observational standpoint and not in absolute terms."[18]

So, it's not easy to figure out who said what and how we got to this spot. However, we have to do the best we can. Learning our history is our best shot at not repeating a wrong behavior; it just takes some digging around to figure out which behavior was good and which was not.

All of this takes more study, but at least now you know the basics that have caused a rift between science and faith, and that it didn't have to be this way—which means we can change it moving forward.

_____

■ Parent Primer #2: Why the Fight Goes On

The facts that science and faith are fighting over are complicated. There have been bad feelings and wrongdoings and fear and also genuine loyalty to the pursuit of truth. It's hard to disentangle which are the actual stumbling blocks that keep science and faith on opposite sides of the street.

"I'm fully convinced that the widespread views in the evangelical world that simply refuse to accommodate in any serious way to contemporary scientific consensus are not just wrong, but they're wrong for Christian reasons," said evangelical scholar Mark Noll.[19] Noll elaborates in his book *Scandal of the Evangelical Mind* his dissatisfaction with how his Christian contemporaries are handling the science and faith debate. The same sentiment has sprouted in the science community.

"I don't deny [Dawkins's] right to be an atheist," said theoretical physicist and atheist Freeman Dyson about fellow scientist and atheist Richard Dawkins, "but I think he does a great deal of harm when he publicly says that in order to be a scientist, you have to be an atheist. . . . The fact is that many of my friends are much more religious than I am and are first-rate scientists. There's absolutely nothing that stops you from being both."[20]

However, the twenty-first century has introduced sharper, stronger, more acrimonious conversation from the science side of the street in the form of "new atheists." The term was coined by *Wired* contributing editor Gary Wolf, who wrote, "The New Atheists will not let us off the hook simply because we are not doctrinaire believers. They condemn not just belief in God but *respect* for belief in God."[21]

New atheists present arguments much the same as their contemporaries of previous centuries, yet with a surgical strike that religion is not merely irrational and unscientific but dangerous.

That circles us back to how this chapter began, except that was about Christians calling scientists dangerous. Now each group has factions that think the other is not just wrong but contemptible.

That contempt has gone beyond disagreements all the way to practically a moral standoff. It has resulted in something of an impasse to basic civil discourse in recent years. Social scientists have begun investigating what drives that kind of polarization, and a word has emerged: disgust.[22] More than being afraid of one another's ideas, modern people are disgusted with those who disagree with us.

That might sound like a dramatic guillotine drop on the debate surrounding science and faith, but it doesn't have to be. We are Christians. Our Scriptures and belief structures do not allow us to be disgusted with people, at least not in that way. Be mad, sure. Disagree, yes. But our marching orders are that love motivates our way, not disgust.

Which is to say, this generation of kids and parents can be agents of improving the relationship between science and faith, effective immediately by simply getting our own bad attitudes in check.

Our kids may respond to that idea with something like, "What about those science folks over there? Are they planning to dial down their bad attitude about Christians?" We parents can tell them: get on with your own business, kids; what they do or do not do is not on your to-do list (John 21:20–22). If Jesus does not play the "But what about them?" game, then neither shall we.

———

HONEST ANSWERS Q&A

Why the Fight Goes On

The run-up to the current-day science-versus-faith debate was really bumpy. But does it seem weird that we still haven't found a way to make it better? Why haven't we? Is it impossible? What is the real problem that prevents us from making the discussion of faith and science more productive? And can we do anything to help? Because dodging church questions in school and dodging science questions in church seems like . . . not really what Jesus had in mind.

1. **Which side is to blame for this science-versus-faith rivalry?**
   A. The faith side. So says a church leader who is not happy with how Christians handle the science-versus-faith debate. He says we believers simply refuse to work with good science right in front of our faces and that's "not just wrong, but . . . wrong for *Christian reasons*."[23]
   B. The science side. So says a science leader who is not happy with how scientists say only atheists (people who say there's no proof that God exists) can be good scientists. He says an atheist who says this does "a great deal of harm when he publicly says that in order to be a scientist, you have to be an atheist. . . . The fact is that many of my friends are much more religious than I am and are first-rate scientists. There's absolutely nothing that stops you from being both."[24]
   C. Both of the above.
      Answer: C
      Both sides of the issue have contributed problems, blindness, and unfair judgments.

2. **If an atheist is someone who says there's no proof that God is God, then what's a "*new* atheist"?**

   "New atheist" is a phrase developed in the last decade or so that describes atheists who condemn "not just belief in God but *respect* for belief in God."[25] New atheists suggest not only that religion is irrational and unscientific but that it is also dangerous.

3. **True or False: New atheists sound more terrifying than anything that's ever been part of the science-versus-faith debate.**
   - True! That sounds terrible for Christians!
   - False. That sentiment is not new, except previously it's been Christians saying that about scientists rather than the other way around.

   Answer: Actually, true *and* false.

   While it is true that being treated as dangerous is terrible for Christians and disrespectful to God, our forefathers once said that people claiming the earth rotates around the sun must "indeed confess that the devil possess them."[26] The lesson here? Stop vilifying (creating villains out of) each other. It's mean and also distracting from the pursuit of God's actual truth, materially and spiritually.

4. **What is a practical way to keep from vilifying people who disagree with us about issues within the science-versus-faith debate?**

   Think about this: in our family, we understand that believing in the truth of God's Word does not stand us in opposition to the truth of God's creation. If certain details of God's Word do not seem to match certain details of God's physical creation, in this house we do not panic about that or seek a villain to blame; we talk about it.

5. **What if someone on the science side of the debate is vilifying us on the faith side? What if they don't play by the same rules?**

It's reasonable to want the other side to dial down their bad attitude if that's what we're doing, but that is not on us to decide. We get on with our business and what they do or do not do is not on our to-do list.

If it makes you feel better, Peter asked the same kind of thing to Jesus, so you're not alone. However, Jesus shut him down (John 21:20–22). So if Jesus does not play the "but what about them?" game, neither shall we. After all, we are trying to turn away wrath, not drum it up, and that takes commitment to having a certain kind of soft answer, not a mean one (Prov. 15:1).

CHAPTER 8

Dissension Within Both Ranks

■ Parent Primer #1: The Unified Voice of Science That Wasn't

CHRISTIANS CAN BEGIN to feel like the science (and secular philosophy) side of the street has got it all together while Christians are scrambling to stand in common consensus even within church circles, but that's not really the case. We parents can convey to our kids that neither side of this science-versus-faith debate has an ironclad, unified voice.

For instance, most of us hear up-and-coming how-science-makes-sense-of-the-world theories that our kids are being taught in school. A recent theory under discussion is a multiverse. Which is what, exactly?

Nobel-prize-winning physicist Steven Weinberg says that, in short, there is no theory of a multiverse. "The theory would be speculative, but we don't even have a theory in which that speculation is mathematically realized."[1]

Okay. Let's leave that alone for the moment and instead get the current consensus on the most basic question of the material world. As in, is this it? Do scientists (and secular philosophers) say anything exists outside time, or is the material world all there is?

On that question too, answers vary.

Centuries ago, Plato thought yes; Aristotle thought no. Plato introduced the idea of "being" (that which is complete and exists outside time) versus "becoming" (which is us, on earth, still under construction). Aristotle came along to say, nope, sorry, what exists is what I see.[2]

Centuries later, that debate rages on.

"I don't think one should underestimate the fix we're in," says Weinberg. "That in the end, we will not be able to explain the world. . . . We will always be left with a question why the laws of nature are what they are rather than some other laws. I don't see any way out of that."[3]

One distinguished rationalist philosopher and atheist, famous for his commitment to "follow the argument wherever it leads," found that his explanation for how the world works, after decades of thinking otherwise, was, well, *God*.

"I now believe there is a God," writes Antony Flew in his last book, *There Is a God*, after deciding there was a Creator after all.[4]

After having helped set the agenda for atheism for half a century, Flew changed his mind.[5] Why? Essentially, he came to the conclusion as a result of these three questions:

1. How did nature come to be?
2. How did life originate from nonlife?
3. How did the universe come into existence?

Flew summarizes his "conversion" like this: "I now believe that the universe was brought into existence by an infinite Intelligence."[6]

Our kids should know that this is not a new argument.

What *is* new is that this renowned atheist came to such a conclusion as this: "I believe that this universe's intricate laws manifest what scientists have called the Mind of God. I believe that life and reproduction originate in a divine Source."[7]

Another modern philosopher has a similar sentiment.

Former Yale Law School dean Anthony Kronman spent most of his life making sense of human existence based strictly on the material world, borrowing from Max Weber's philosophy. "[Weber] recommended a kind of stoical resignation. . . . He said, 'God has vanished. You may believe or not, that's up to you, but as a public matter, gone, gone, gone . . . accept that fact as your fate,'" said Kronman. "And for a long time in my twenties and thirties and forties and fifties, I said, 'That's *right* and I can live a stoical life of that kind.'

"And then it just stopped working for me," Kronman said. "The meaning of my commitments, my attachments, my worldly vocation couldn't for me be ultimately secured in a way that would be . . . personally convincing unless I could relate all of my life to something that is not touched by time."[8]

So, let's review from the science side of the street. Explanation of how the world came into existence from a material, scientific view? Not exactly sure yet. Is the material world all there is, or does something exist outside time? Jury's still out. So much so that a Yale philosopher headed over to the Scriptures to articulate what science and philosophy could not, because of, as we quoted to our kids in an earlier chapter, his "bone-deep belief in the infinite value of the individual . . . that's a biblical idea, invention, discovery, however you wish to characterize it."[9]

All of that might sound like Christian belief, but our kids should know that Kronman is not claiming to be a Christian. Neither is Flew. They're simply working out their worldview and discovering, to the degree of truth they were seeking, that God's creation speaks for itself (Job 12:7–10; Rom. 1:20).

———

HONEST ANSWERS Q&A

The Unified Voice of Science That Wasn't

We love God; we love being Christians and living the life of a believer.

Yet, on the matter of science versus faith, do you ever get the idea that science is just a little bit more *together*? More *together* together, like whatever makes up the group called "science," that group all agrees, and they see the world the same way, and they love to talk about the stuff they're working on because they're a crew, in it *together*. Not just now, but since the beginning of time because the people on their team are huge, like Plato and Aristotle, and everybody's proud of everybody.

Would you be surprised to hear that it's not exactly like that?

Well, surprise! It's not exactly like that.

In fact, it's a lot like any other group that has a common idea, but has lots and lots of areas that are still under construction. Let's talk about some of that now.

1. Which of the following is true?
   A. Scientists have got it all together within science ranks; there is a clear voice of consensus (agreement) on all matters of science.
   B. Christians have got it all together within the church body; there is a clear voice of consensus (agreement) on all matters of faith.
   C. Neither of the above.
   Answer: C
   Scientists observe the material world and agree with other scientists on lots of things. Christians read Scripture and agree with other Christians on lots of things. However, everybody's still working out a lot of details. This is simply the process of how humans beings learn. We learn something,

test it, grow in it, understand it more, update old learning as needed, repeat. Nobody has a corner on the market of "knows it all."

2. **What's an example of a scientist saying that science does not "know it all"?**

Steven Weinberg, a Nobel prize–winning physicist, a guy who would know it all if ever there was, says this: "I don't think one should underestimate the fix we're in: that in the end, we will not be able to explain the world. . . . We will always be left with a question why the laws of nature are what they are rather than some other laws. I don't see any way out of that."[10]

3. **Do scientists admit that everything on earth is not all there is?**
   A. Yes! All the way back to Plato, who believed in the idea of "being" (that which is complete and exists outside time) versus "becoming" (which is us, on earth, still under construction).[11]
   B. Don't be ridiculous, no! Aristotle made it clear that what exists is what he sees.[12]
   C. Depends who you ask.
   Answer: C
   In science circles, this debate started before Jesus was even born, and the debate rages on still today.

4. **Name one example of a scientist today who would answer "Yes!" to that question.**

Antony Flew, a distinguished atheist who is famous for setting the there-is-no-God agenda for half a century, said the following:
   - "I now believe that the universe was brought into existence by an infinite Intelligence."[13]
   - "I believe that this universe's intricate laws manifest [show] what scientists have called the Mind of God. I believe that life and reproduction originate in a divine Source."[14]

5. **When a scientist admits that there is something more than just what we see, does that mean they have faith in God?**

Alas, no. Sometimes they're simply working out their world-view and discovering that, to the degree of truth they were seeking, God's creation speaks for itself (Job 12:7–10; Rom. 1:20).

6. **Wouldn't it be nice if scientists followed that up with leaning on Scripture?**

Actually, a Yale philosopher began to do just that. He headed over to the Scriptures to explain something that science and philosophy were failing to explain for him. He said, "My deep, deep, my bone-deep belief in the infinite value of the individual . . . that's a biblical idea, invention, discovery—however you wish to characterize it."[15]

■ Parent Primer #2: The Unified Voice of Faith That Wasn't

Christians wanting to present a united front to kids' questions about science may still be in a bit of a quandary. We simply do not all see the Scriptures speaking on science matters in the same way.

For instance, according to scientists, humans share more than 90 percent of genetic sequencing with chimpanzees and subsequently evolved into the human beings we are today.[16] What's the consensus among Christians on what to tell our kids about that?

It depends who you ask.

According to Asbury Theological Seminary's Ben Witherington, there are five categories (oversimplified here for the sake of outlining) Christians fall into on this topic.[17]

1. People are created (no evolution); the earth is about 6,000 years old.
2. People are created (no evolution); the earth is WAY older than 6,000 years old.
3. Yes, evolution happened, but not to humans; humans were uniquely created in the image of God.
4. Yes, evolution happened, including to humans, but, Witherington notes, "At some point God put a 'soul' into human beings (that's what the image of God is)." Adam and Eve existed, and when Paul refers to Adam, he is referring to a literal, historical character (Rom. 5:12–21; 1 Cor. 11:8, 11–12).
5. Yes, evolution happened, but Adam and Eve are allegorical, not historical characters, and when Paul refers to Adam, he is referring to the story of Adam, not a historical character. This is called "theistic evolution."

Arguments within theological circles are nothing new. Think about forefathers of faith George Whitefield and John Wesley: each was convinced by his own reading of Scripture and yet they disagreed over the idea of predestination. After their major split, the

Methodist denomination was credited to Wesley while the evangelical strand of Protestantism, à la the revivalist Great Awakening of the
mid-eighteenth century, followed Whitefield. However, the two are
rumored to have remained friends behind the scenes.[18]

Way before Wesley and Whitefield came the apostles Peter and
Paul, who fought over the theology of who should save a seat for whom
at lunch.

As the story goes, long after he should have known better, Peter
decided not to eat with his new Christian Gentile friends in order to
save face in front of visiting old-guard religious Jewish buddies (Gal.
2:11–13). Enter Paul, who called Peter out on his hypocritical behavior and, in front of the whole crowd, told him to cut it out.

Welcome to the church's "iron-sharpens-iron" kind of love (Prov.
27:17). Confronting one another *is* love. Peter and Paul maintained
their friendship, as we see Peter later writing lovingly and admiringly
about Paul (2 Peter 3:15–16).

However, church conflicts didn't always work out that cleanly.

Case in point: Paul and Barnabas. After preaching and ministering
for some time, the apostle Paul wanted to go back to check on believers in the various towns that he and Barnabas had visited. Barnabas
wanted to take John Mark (also called Mark) with them, but Paul
did not. Mark had been problematic before, and Paul didn't want to
bother with him again. Barnabas disagreed. So Paul and Barnabas
broke up over it (Acts 15:36–41).

After some time, Paul eventually worked with Mark again (2 Tim.
4:11), though it's unclear how well Paul and Barnabas patched things
up (1 Cor. 9:5). We parents of this generation are trying to minimize
friendship fractures in the first place. Some of our contemporary
church leaders do not want these fractures either.

Mark Noll, whom we mentioned earlier, purposely maintains
friendships with Christian leaders who think differently than he
does. For instance, Noll wrote a foreword for the book of his friend
John Piper, a young earth advocate, in which Noll acknowledged
their differences: "My book says a few things about science (especially

evolution) that many of John's appreciative readers, and maybe John himself, might not approve."[19]

Then Noll complimented his friend's book and commended it to the reader, writing, "The point of Christian learning is to understand God's two books—Scripture and the world—and, with that understanding, to glorify God. The pages before you communicate that point very well."[20]

This art of disagreeing *agreeably* is not born; it is built—out of habit, out of discourse, out of friendship, out of fundamental respect for the process of critical thought and the dignity of people, if not particular agreement with their conclusions. If Christians cannot have consensus on where exactly we stand on matters of science, at least we can have conversation.

HONEST ANSWERS Q&A

The Unified Voice of Faith That Wasn't

Do you ever feel like you can't share what you actually think about science while you're at church? Because your impression is that everybody at church thinks the same thing about science? And what they think is more correct than what you think? In fact, it's probably more biblical? And you saying whatever it is you're thinking would basically get Jesus mad at you?

Would you be surprised to hear that lots of people at church are still working through what they think about science? And also, they might not actually know what other Christians really think about matters of science. It's not easy to discuss, because nobody wants to make Paul and Moses and *Jesus* mad, and nobody wants other church members mad either.

However, we want to start sharing about these things a little more freely, so we can learn from each other. Being a member of the church body of Christ is one of the most wonderful gifts we can imagine. That kind of community is really helpful when we need a safe place to have hard conversations. Let's talk about that today.

1. **Do all Christians have the same answers to questions that arise around the science-versus-faith debate?**
   A. Yes! We all agree! About everything!
   B. No. That's what it means to be Christian—you make up your own mind about everything based on you and God.
   C. Christians have several common thoughts on science, yet even though we hold a high view of Scripture, we sometimes come to different conclusions about what God is saying through his Word.

Answer: C

One example where Christians have a similar core thought is that God created people in his image (Gen. 1:27), yet Christians differ on how to explain a scientific claim that over 90 percent of our human genetic sequencing is like that of chimpanzees.

2. **What are the five main views Christians have on the subject of evolution?**[21]
   - People are created (no evolution); the earth is about 6,000 years old.
   - People are created (no evolution); the earth is WAY older than 6,000 years old.
   - Yes, evolution happened, but not to humans; humans were uniquely created in the image of God.
   - Yes, evolution happened, including to humans, but, Witherington notes, "At some point God put a 'soul' into human beings (that's what the image of God is)." Adam and Eve existed, and when Paul refers to Adam, he is referring to a literal, historical character (Rom. 5:12–21; 1 Cor. 11:8, 11–12).
   - Yes, evolution happened, but Adam and Eve are allegorical, not historical characters, and when Paul refers to Adam, he is referring to the story of Adam, not a historical character. This is called "theistic evolution."

3. **Why would Christians listen to people who don't believe in God in order to understand God's creation of human beings?**

   First of all, that 90-percent-shared-with-chimps genetic sequencing number came from a famous genome project run by a Christian[22]—a very public Christian who preaches his faith in Jesus often and proudly.[23] That said, just because some scientists aren't believers doesn't mean that God can't use them to reveal truth. Lots of people in the Bible revealed truths about God even though they didn't believe in God. (One example is King Abimelek, who soundly schooled Abraham on how God felt about Abraham being shady and pawning off Sarah as his sister in Genesis 20:4–18.)

4. How can we represent Christ in a positive way when we argue over basic things?

People in the church do not agree on everything—that's nothing new. Look at Peter and Paul. After they'd helped a new group of people become Christians, Peter wanted to ditch them because his old friends, who were more established believers, were coming to town. Paul told him to cut it out (Gal. 2:11–13). The fact that Peter and Paul argued is actually really helpful for us. We learn not to play favorites or act differently around important people. But the argument also shows us that disagreements happen and it isn't the end of the world. In fact, later Peter said nice stuff about Paul, so we know they maintained a good friendship (2 Peter 3:15–16).

5. True or False: Arguments between Christians in the Bible were always resolved quickly.

Answer: False.

An example is the fight between Paul and Barnabas. Here are the details:

- After preaching and ministering for some time, the apostle Paul wanted to go back to check on believers in the various towns that he and Barnabas had visited.
- Barnabas wanted to take John Mark (aka just Mark) with them, but Paul did not. Mark had been problematic before, and Paul didn't want to bother with him again.
- Barnabas disagreed. So much so that the two went their separate ways over it (Acts 15:36–41).
- Paul did eventually work with Mark again (2 Tim. 4:11), and he fleetingly mentions Barnabas later on, though it's hard to get a read on their relationship (1 Cor. 9:5).

Let's try to prevent our disagreements from damaging our friendships in the first place.

6. Are there any modern examples of Christians disagreeing about the science-versus-faith debate but still staying friends?

Yes! There's a church leader who writes lots of books and is very vocal about the right way Christians should be handling the science-versus-faith debate. Still, he endorsed his friend's book, even though they disagree. The church leader was honest, saying, "My book says a few things about science (especially evolution) that many of John's appreciative readers, and maybe John himself, might not approve."[24] But he still showed up for his friend, supported his book, and complimented him.

This art of disagreeing *agreeably* is not born; it is built. It takes training and practice. If Christians cannot agree on where exactly we stand on all matters of science, at least we can have conversation.

CHAPTER 9

Motivation Is Key

■ Parent Primer #1: Speak the Truth

SCIENTISTS ARE NOT inherently trying to put God out of a job. As we have learned here, there are scientists (and philosophers) who are not afraid to announce new observations, even if those observations look complementary to ideas coming out of the faith side of the street.

Can we parents say the same? Especially since the motivation Christians should have for following an argument where it leads is one thing: to know God more. If we stick with that incentive, what have we to gain by coming into a science-versus-faith conversation wearing our fight faces? We actually have a lot to lose, because we'd miss meaningful insights into our God's creativity on display throughout the cosmos and his simultaneous attention to ordering even the infinitesimal elements of the material world. His precision is almost beyond description, yet we know lots and lots about it, thanks to science.

Our motivation to know God more calls forth in us one behavior in particular: telling the truth. Truth-telling is especially important when it comes to Scripture and helping our kids see when the Bible is making absolute claims about the material world and when it is not.

For instance, nobody assumes the sky is a *raqiya`*, the Hebrew word for a hard dome that holds water at bay behind it (Gen. 1:6–8). Why?

Because running repeatable experiments on the modern, material world has given us an understanding of some of its building blocks, and a *raqiya*ˋ is not one of them.[1]

However, what's a parent who holds a high view of Scripture to say about this? If we read *raqiya*ˋ as something ancient writers observed, rather than an absolute, are we downgrading Scripture to the status of "interesting—but primitive"? Because of all things we parents wish most *not to do*, downgrading the Bible ranks at the top.

We'd rather start selling our kids on *raqiya*ˋ with a straight face. No way can we downgrade the Scriptures. They've been our lifelines to God.

However, Alister McGrath, who holds a doctorate from Oxford University in molecular biophysics, says Christianity is "not about running away from evidence or proof, it's about embracing them."[2] Is it possible to embrace the proofs of science without being disloyal to God and his Scripture, which we love very, very much? Some scientists who are also Christians say yes, absolutely. For instance, philosopher of science Dr. Stephen C. Meyer has claimed that there is compelling data that DNA was originated by a designer with a purpose.[3]

That will resonate with our kids. First they'll hear blah, blah, blah . . . then they'll remember: this is not what they were taught about Darwin's evolution in science class. Darwin said that although all things are in fact designed, it's by chance.

In other words, submitting passively to initial science claims is not what the situation calls for. Scientists do not passively submit to one another, so why would Christians be compelled to?

Submitting to Scripture is also not passive. As discussed in prior chapters, Scripture is to be adored, but not at the expense of engaging it. To that end, Christians can play the Augustine of Hippo trump card that we discussed: watching as a theory is vetted but reserving our final verdict while observing how the argument progresses.

As in this cause-versus-chance debate, theoretical physicist and atheist Freeman Dyson, having examined the evidence from the vantage point of a scientist, made this claim: "The more I examine the universe and the details of its architecture, the more evidence I find that the universe in some sense must have known we were coming."[4]

We Christian parents want to say, "Yes, Dr. Dyson, yes. Someone did."

The more we acknowledge the truth as it presents itself in the material world, possibly the more the Dr. Dysons of the world will care about and receive our truthful witness about the Savior of the world.

So will our kids.

———————

Speak the Truth

All this conversation about the science and faith debate has us thinking, Have we discussed what we as a family are motivated by when we talk about science or Scripture? Our motivation is to know God more. Do you know that to do that, we need to find, listen to, and tell the truth? That sounds obvious, and yet we have to be a little brave to say what is true about science and Scripture. We do not need to be scared of the truth. In fact, Jesus says he *is* the truth (John 14:6). That means God's got this. So let's explore some truths in relation to the faith-versus-science discussion.

1. **Which of the following is a true statement about scientists?**
   A. Scientists are not necessarily trying to put God out of a job or prove him to be wrong.
   B. There are scientists who are not afraid to follow the argument wherever it leads, even if that means heading toward what some recognize as faith.
   C. Investigation is not always about ego. It's about learning, growing, and exploring.
   D. Some scientists really want to stick it to God and would be thrilled if people would just stop talking about God already.
   E. All of the above.
   Answer: E
   We need to refrain from coming into a science-versus-faith conversation with our fight faces on. Talking with people who have really scientific minds is a chance to learn a lot about God's material world. Enjoy. Also, if their conversation turns dark on God, that's on them. We will behave how

we choose to behave or how we are led by the Holy Spirit to behave. That will be purposeful, not drawn into an argument in reaction to somebody else getting on our nerves with what they say about God, even though they bug us because we love God very, very much.

2. **Does having a high view of Scripture mean we have to assume every claim in the Bible about the material world is an absolute?**

No. Of course not. Have you heard of *raqiya*`? It's the Genesis 1:6–8 "firmament" (KJV), and in Hebrew it means a dome. A hard one. Holding water at bay above it. That was evidently how the ancient writers observed the sky back in days of yore.

3. **If we do not hold every comment in the Bible about the material world as an absolute, does that mean we have downgraded Scripture to "interesting—but primitive"?**
    A. No.
    B. No way.
    C. Not at all.
    D. Not even a little.
    E. Nope, *nein* (no in German), *non* (no in French), *nej* (no in Swedish), no ma'am (no politely), No! (no impolitely).
    F. All of the above.
    Answer: F

So, no; the answer is *no*. We cling to the Scriptures like the life raft that they are. They keep us tethered to the truth about God. They keep us from swirling off into nowhere in our faith, in our mental well-being, in our capacity to love and *function*. No, the fact that we understand that the sky is not hard like a dome does not in any way indicate that we downgrade the Scriptures. No. It simply means that we use our understanding of history and ancient times to guide our reading of Scripture. (Remember all that from part 1?)

4. **What is an example of a scientific claim that once alarmed Christians but is now less alarming?**

   Philosopher of science Dr. Stephen C. Meyer claims that there is now compelling data that DNA was designed with purpose.[5]

   After you hear "blah, blah, blah . . . looks like things got their start by a designer with a purpose," then what do you notice? This is not what you were taught about evolution in science class. An important point the evolution guy (Darwin) made is that although all things are designed, it's by chance.

   Dr. Meyer is making a case that it's not by chance but rather the result of a designer with a purpose in mind.

5. **Why does it matter that the world was started on purpose rather than by chance?**

   A. It shows Christians that the idea that God made the world is not only part of our faith, but it's a demonstrable idea with evidence in the material world (what we see and touch). That's an example of God's material world observationally aligning with his written Word.

   B. It illustrates the Augustine idea that if Christians refrain from rushing in with rash things to say and instead allow science to be a process under construction, we can get out of the way of God's material world demonstrating God's truths for itself (Job 12:7–10; Rom. 1:20).

   C. Both of the above.

   Answer: C

■ **Parent Primer #2: Sharing Is Messy. Do It Anyway.**

If our kids have the sentiment that God is boss of both sides of this debate, and if they check their attitude, avoiding disdain for people who disagree with them, can our kids count on smooth sailing in their conversations around science and faith?

Alas, not likely.

Basic peer review and discussion create tension. That's how the system works; there is no way around it. We parents will have to train up our kids: when talking a thing out is hard, that's not a sign we are doing it wrong. That's a sign we are actually doing it at all.

Let's use an illustration to make this point. We can look at a discussion between two scientists who disagree on a trending topic in science circles called a "selfish gene."

In his book we mentioned earlier, Antony Flew shoots down fellow atheist Richard Dawkins's notion of a "selfish gene," meant to explain, as Dawkins said, that we "are machines created by our genes."[6]

Flew states that if Dawkins's selfish gene notion were true, there would be no reason to "teach generosity and altruism" as Dawkins says we should, since "no eloquence can move programmed robots."[7]

Dawkins, on the other hand, says the survival of genes, such as those genes that behave altruistically, "make its bearer behave altruistically" via kinship and strong survival bodies.[8]

Let the record show, the conversation wasn't contentious per se, but it certainly wasn't friendly either. This gives us parents a scripted dialogue that makes a point for our kids: if someone shoots down their ideas on a matter like Flew did to Dawkins, our kids will need to choose not to wilt and wither on the vine. Smart, civil discourse benefits the body of knowledge on any particular matter, even if we haven't convinced the other person of our point. That all parties do not agree is sometimes helpful for outsiders trying to make up *their* minds.

Here is a small data point that our kids can use to dip a toe into the science-versus-faith conversation. Augustine of Hippo came to the conclusion that there are "two 'moments' in creation: a primary act of origination and a continuing process of providential guidance."[9]

In other words, Augustine wrote about God bringing "everything into existence in a single moment of creation," explains McGrath. Yet he says that according to Augustine, "the created order is not static. God endowed it with the capacity to develop."[10]

We parents can ask our kids questions like: What do we think about this idea? In what way is it a high view of Scripture? In what ways might this make some Christians hot under the collar? How does one proceed in a conversation if that happens?

We will have the pleasure of leading our kids in how to have intelligent conversations about science and faith. And, before you panic too much, there are loads of resources in the notes section of this book, including dialogues from theologians and scientists who represent a wide range of views. Each has a high view of Scripture.

"What remains for us to discover are all the facts that relate to genuine questions of human well-being," said Sam Harris, one of today's leading "new atheists." "The only tool we need to do that is honest, open inquiry."[11]

Christians wouldn't agree that that's the *only* tool we need, but it is an important one by which we can at the very least have honest, open inquiry regarding the science-versus-faith conversation if we behave as Christians are called, to "act justly and to love mercy and to walk humbly with [our] God" and with each other (Mic. 6:8; Eph. 4:1–4; Col. 1:15–18). We should furthermore present as the least peevish people in the room with the least reflexive answers to questions that are very important to us all. These questions are also of utmost importance to God, who wants to show himself to a world that he loves very, very much.

HONEST ANSWERS Q&A

Sharing Is Messy. Do It Anyway.

Do you think it is easy to share ideas and opinions? Or hard to share them? It may sound like a silly question, but that is easy for some people and hard for others. We're going to talk today about sharing ideas and opinions in a productive way: what to avoid, how to hang in there. We want to warn you that this is tough. Even if sharing ideas comes easy, if someone shoots down a really good idea—especially if it has something to do with our very core, like our faith in God—that can be devastating. However, let this sink in: if it's hard, that doesn't mean we're doing it wrong.

1. **What are two ways we can approach the science-versus-faith debate so that we have smooth sailing in our conversation?**
   A. If we have the understanding that God's boss of both sides of this argument, we'll have smooth sailing, because how can two things from the same Creator be in conflict with each other?
   B. If we keep our attitudes in check, we'll have smooth sailing, because Christians avoid looking down on people who disagree with us.
   C. Neither of the above.
      Answer: C
      Sorry, but smooth sailing is not how this is going to go. The suggestions above will help, no doubt, and will help undo some damage of contentious conversations from the past, and that in fact is how we should proceed as Christians. But basic dialogue about topics that do not fit easily together is going to have tension. Sorry, but that's part of it. Remember, that doesn't mean we're doing it wrong. That means we're doing it, period.

2. **Read through this illustration of how one scientist disagrees with another scientist on a trending scientific topic called the "selfish gene." Don't be concerned with what he says about the topic; focus on how he disagrees with the other scientist.**

   • In his book, Antony Flew shoots down fellow scientist and atheist Richard Dawkins's notion of a "selfish gene," meant to explain, as Dawkins said, that we "are machines created by our genes."[12] Dawkins says the survival of our genes, such as those genes that behave altruistically, "make its bearer behave altruistically" via kinship and strong survival bodies.[13] Basically Dawkins is saying we only help other people to ensure that they will help us.

   • Flew said that if Dawkins's selfish-gene notion were true, there would be no reason to "teach generosity and altruism" as Dawkins says we should, since "no eloquence can move programmed robots."[14]

3. **What can we learn from the above illustration?**
   A. Even scientists disagree about stuff.
   B. Flew didn't say Dawkins wasn't nice or wasn't moral or wasn't whatever. He stuck with one item: according to Flew, Dawkins was wrong.
   C. Flew argued against Dawkins's idea by Dawkins's own standards.
   D. All of the above.
   Answer: D

   Some of these ideas may seem obvious, but many of us have become terrible at having civil discussions! It's as if we've forgotten the basics, like don't drag somebody through the mud to make a point about their point. Also, Flew disagreed with Dawkins by using language and standards that Dawkins also feels are actual standards. That's a good lesson for Christians to keep in mind when using Scripture to demonstrate a point. We should be able to speak to the point the other person is making, not merely repeat a line from Scripture and hope that does the trick (1 Cor. 9:19–22).

4. **Do Christians have any language from historic Christians about the science-versus-faith debate that could be helpful for civil discourse today?**

Here's one to consider. That forefather we keep mentioning, Augustine of Hippo, came to the conclusion that there are "two 'moments' in creation: a primary act of origination and a continuing process of providential guidance."[15] In other words, Augustine thought that what God created came into existence under the hand of God but continued to change and develop after that.[16]

Let's discuss that as a family. What do we think Augustine meant by a continuing process of development in creation? In what way is this consistent with a high view of Scripture? In what ways might this make some Christians nervous? How does one proceed in a conversation if that happens?

5. **What are good ways Christians can behave as we are called, to "act justly and to love mercy and to walk humbly" with God and with each other (Mic. 6:8; Eph. 4:1–4; Col. 1:15–18)?**
   - Do what it takes to have honest, open conversations.
   - Behave as the least peevish (testy, touchy, grouchy) people in the room.
   - Have the least reactive (not thought-through, jargon-filled) answers to questions.

6. **What if we just don't have the personality for discussing science-versus-faith matters like these?**

That's fine. We all have different gifts. We just need to be sure we're not letting fear be the boss of us. So if someone shoots down our idea on a matter, as Flew was doing to Dawkins, we will need to choose to understand the topic for ourselves and not to just hide away.

PART FOUR

WHAT IS CHURCH *SUPPOSED* TO LOOK LIKE?

INTRODUCTION FOR PARENTS

A TEN-YEAR-OLD BOY invited his buddy over to his house during a family party that came to a slight pause when the food arrived. Someone grabbing plates loudly asked the group, "Who wants to bless this food in prayer?" The buddy raised his hand to volunteer, and then posed this question, "Can I say a Catholic one?"

Kids' candor tends to come through at the most public moments. The punch line typically is the parents, a tiny bit slack-jawed, having neglected to give kids credit for their ability to notice what's happening around them.

In this case, they're noticing that churches look like slight variations on a common theme. Yet kids are not sure what that common theme is. And how do they navigate that publicly? Kids need instruction on how to wrap their arms around the exact commonality that matters most among churches.

They see friends who have Advent calendars at Christmas or give up treats for Lent before Easter or can't be on the lacrosse team because it plays on Sundays. Also, some don't go to church but still use familiar language like Jesus, love, and Bible.

Kids are at a loss as to how to make sense of these differences. Basically, they're not sure of this: What exactly is church *supposed* to look like anyway?

One resource for a great answer to that might be surprising.

The church is "a world that's organized around a particular mood, the mood of agape love," said Harvard professor of philosophy Sean Kelly. "It seems to me that that mood wasn't really around until we had the community that was organized around Jesus."[1]

We want our kids to know about that church—a body of believers arranged around Christ, who willingly died, resurrected, and transformed the whole community into people who unashamedly love others because they were loved first so comprehensively and conclusively by God. The collective throng of worldwide support and encouragement and clarity and responsibility that goes with that is what we want to download into our kids. We also want to avoid the unfortunate mob mentality that overtook our beloved church body at pivotal points in history.

That an agnostic academic from Harvard testifies to the agape love (the love from God to us) of the church is handy messaging we parents can use to inform our kids, especially now that young believers, according to the Pew Research Center, are leaving the church en masse, having had it with the sanctimony of some believers.[2]

We parents may not have the jurisdiction to reverse all issues around the latest Pew findings, but we can help the people in our own home. We can answer their questions honestly and effectively (read: short and snappy, without omitting the bad stuff).

We might be a little nervous about discussing why we have so many denominations. And we may feel slightly terrified to mention the fine, upstanding church leaders from back in the day who raged bloody conquests in the name of religion. Come to think of it, what will we possibly have to say to our kids about that?

Plenty. We parents will have plenty to say.

Each element of church history is one part of a very big story. Believers belong to a centuries-strong global church that actually pivoted the trajectory of modern civilization toward, well, civility. "The individual morality of conscience, human rights, and democracy, is the direct heir to the Judaic ethic of justice and the Christian ethic of love," said world-renowned atheist Jürgen Habermas. "Everything else is just idle postmodern talk."[3]

Our kids can get idle postmodern talk anywhere. Here, we want to give our kids their roots as a Christian community. To do that, we will tackle this short but mighty task list about the church:

1. Its setup. We'll run through how first-century believers gathered for worship and handled community and how subsequent

church leaders laid out the church arrangements that we recognize today.

2. Its breakups. We'll pinpoint where the body of believers split into denominations. We'll give our kids a snapshot of what happened and why it happened, and encourage them to be charitable in their response to all of this, because the body of Christ can sometimes lean a little more on body and less on Christ than we'd like to admit.

3. Its future. We'll sound this rallying cry: do not count out the church. Yes, the body has needed course corrections (for posterity, we will point out a few of the worst), but the church is built with a spine of steel, courtesy of the one true God.

Anybody panicked? Of course we are. Let's get started anyway in hopes of giving our kids a shot at knowing God just a little bit better.

CHAPTER 10

The Church's Setup

■ Parent Primer #1: In the Beginning . . .

To GET A solid foundation, let's start at the beginning. While we cannot pinpoint the exact worship rundown of the first church gatherings, early Christians likely met in private homes (Acts 2:46; 16:40; 18:7; Philem. 2), at the beginning of the week (Acts 20:7; 1 Cor. 16:2), when they had a ceremonial meal and Communion (1 Cor. 10:16–17; 11:20–34), taught Scripture, and sang songs (Acts 2:42).

Structure was added as the church grew, which is where we parents may start to sweat. Scripture outlines roles like elders, who must be "blameless," who must be hospitable and not have a temper, and whose kids had better be believers (Titus 1:6–9). All that can froth us into a good panic because an assembly with that kind of perfect leadership sounds hard to come by.

Maybe we could be elders? But there's that word "blameless." And the temper issue. That our kids are believers is the easy one—just ask our tween, "You believe, right? Right? *Right?*"

In other words, we can tell our kids that our church community matters very, very much, and it is measured not by perfect leaders or followers but by its spreading of a specific bit of good news. It all started when an eyewitness woman told the apostles that Jesus, who died for our sins, had risen victorious over sin and death (John 20:18).

Wait. Scratch that. There are two camps on this. See how fun this is already!

Another camp says the spreading of Jesus's good news did not actually start until a month(ish) later, when a room full of 120 of Jesus's staunchest supporters was awash with the Holy Spirit, so much so that tongues of fire appeared over their heads (Acts 2).

Either way, the events around Jesus's resurrection were monumental. The apostle Peter marked this juncture in history by quoting the prophet Joel's message from God: "Even on my servants, both men and women, I will pour out my Spirit" (Acts 2:18).

Did he ever.

The early believers were overwhelmingly joyful and expressive. Who could blame them? They were coming off a heritage wherein their Israelite ancestors took sputtering starts and stops with God, with story lines that included wandering through the wilderness. A lot.

Mercifully, they were rescued from Egypt, and later rescued from exile in Babylon and Persia, and their plans to rebuild the temple were rescued, and overall rescue was a very big thing. Now they were bearing witness to Jesus's resurrection, which rescued the world from the sting of death itself. It was time to spread the good news.

Hello, church.

However, the first steps were not easy. Jesus's dying for us sounded strange to people back then; they needed help reasoning and figuring out this idea of a Savior (Acts 17:17–20), which was a lot for the early church to wrap their heads around.

To dig into it all, they worked together, with Paul regularly thanking "co-workers" by name in his letters—Timothy, Priscilla, Titus, and more (Rom. 16:3; 2 Cor. 8:23; 1 Thess. 3:2).

The word *church* or *gathering* (Greek word *ekklesia*) came to mean for them gathering together and encouraging one another to love and do good deeds (Heb. 10:24–25). "So Christ himself gave the apostles, the prophets, the evangelists, the pastors and teachers, to equip his people for works of service, so that the body of Christ may be built up" (Eph. 4:11–12).

They baptized new believers promptly and also made a huge shift to a new idea that God did not live in a temple but inside us. "Don't you know that you yourselves are God's temple and that God's Spirit dwells in your midst?" (1 Cor. 3:16).

At risk of torture and death, these men and women used their gifts to doggedly express the good news while resisting the culture at that time from corrupting their message.

Alas, little by little, corruption crept in anyway.

HONEST ANSWERS Q&A

In the Beginning . . .

Perhaps some of your friends have Advent calendars at Christmas, or give up treats for Lent before Easter, or can't be on the lacrosse team because it plays on Sundays. Also, some don't go to church and some do, and perhaps you've asked before what church differences even matter. And was it all supposed to look like *this*?

It's a great question and one we don't spend a lot of time talking about. We're usually focused on faith or the Bible, but getting a grip on what church is meant to be is a good idea, since it's not always going to be obvious just by looking around.

Let's be honest. The church today is working through a few growing pains. But the church isn't a fragile, inflexible thing that will shatter at the smallest problem. It's been going through growing pains since . . . well, now we come to think of it, pretty much all the way along. You'll see when we run through for you what the very first church was like. You might be surprised.

And by the way, your personal relationship with Jesus is unique and wonderful, but we want to make a point that you are part of something that is bigger than just you and bigger than just our family and even bigger than our community and where we worship. You're part of a centuries-long buildup of a church body. It's an incredible thing to be part of.

1. **What was the first Christian church like?**
   A. Fantastic! Jesus was the lead pastor.
   B. Confusing. And exciting. And a little nerve-racking.
   C. Terrific! Somebody brought leftover manna.
   Answer: B
   First of all, the church is the body of believers in

Christ, which happened *after* Jesus's death and resurrection, so no chance he would have been lead pastor. Also, manna? From Moses and the wilderness, like six hundred pages ago? Plus manna spoiled every day, so no. Which leaves B as the correct answer, which might come as a surprise. Even Jesus's staunchest believers were a little confused about what was going on after his crucifixion.

2. **But at least we can agree about the moment when the spreading of the gospel started, right?**

   Actually, no. There are two main ideas about that:
   - One idea is that the first gospel-spreader was a woman who ran to tell the apostles that Jesus had risen from the dead (John 20:18).
   - Another idea is that the gospel was launched a month(ish) later when 120 of Jesus's best friends, men and women, were filled with the Holy Spirit and then began spreading the "good news" (Acts 2).

3. **What did the first church services look like?**
   - Church members got together at each other's houses.
   - They prayed, sang songs, shared a meal, and read and discussed Scripture (Acts 2:42; 1 Cor. 10:16–17; 11:20–34).

4. **The apostle Paul regularly thanked his church "co-workers" by name in his letters. Here are three of them:**
   - Timothy (1 Thess. 3:2).
   - Priscilla (Rom. 16:3).
   - Titus (2 Cor. 8:23).

5. **Why would Paul call people co-workers? What was such hard work about getting together at people's houses?**

   When Jesus rose from the dead, it was incredibly surprising to even his closest friends. They were poring over the Scriptures (just the Old Testament at that point) and talking about what

Jesus had said, honestly getting their heads around how this all fit together. That took a lot of work. Plus, they were spreading the word about Jesus all over; that included traveling and hosting people who came to town. Plus, they were attending to the needs of the poor.

6. Why didn't Jesus make clear what was going to happen to him? Why did he allow it to be so confusing to his friends?

Jesus did tell them. He told them implicitly (in picture language) and explicitly (flat out, straight up), but his friends simply did not understand. This doesn't mean Jesus felt all hurt and misunderstood that they didn't get it. God is all about relationship and allowing people to come to an understanding of him as the story unfolds and as they walk through life with him.

Read these verses about Nicodemus: John 3:1–21; 19:38–42. The way Jesus explained himself to Nicodemus is a good example of how Jesus used picture language so Nicodemus could start to understand from his own frame of reference. It took Nicodemus some thinking, but in the end he was one of the only ones tending to Jesus's body.

Getting our head around the whole arc of God's story is one reason that we need the church. God making the world, then people sinning, then all the stuff with the Israelites, then the big triumphant Jesus resurrection moment—this takes a lot of unpacking. Doing all that alone? Not great. Thanks to the body of Christ, we don't have to.

7. Isn't the point of Jesus that now we can leave the Old Testament and pour all our focus on the New Testament?

It isn't helpful to yank the climax right out of the story. Jesus is part of this whole long story line, so believe him when he says if you don't get Moses, you're missing something about Jesus.

Remember that verse we noted in earlier chapters, "If you

believed Moses, you would believe me, for he wrote about me. But since you do not believe what he wrote, how are you going to believe what I say?" (John 5:46–47).

Jesus's friends and followers knew about the stories of God's rescue and had an idea that God was coming with a really big rescue and here it was: people were bearing witness to Jesus's resurrection, which rescued the world from the sting of death itself. They had to go back to the Israelite story and reconsider parts they thought would turn out one way but were turning out another. They had to pay attention to things that hadn't seemed as evident before.

8. **Once people understood that Jesus fulfilled the Old Testament Scripture, then why keep rehashing the old story lines?**
   A. Because there are not old story lines and new story lines; they're all *the* story line.
   B. Because there's more to Jesus than birth, death, resurrection. He said important stuff; he did important stuff.
   C. Because New Testament characters made odd comments like, "Does [Jesus] intend to go . . . and teach the Greeks?" (John 7:35), as if the Old Testament does not repeatedly endorse reaching out and welcoming non-Jews as believers (like Rahab, Ruth, Nebuchadnezzar). Their hero Solomon even prayed fervently for "the foreigner who does not belong to your people Israel but has come from a distant land because of your great name" (2 Chron. 6:32).
   D. All of the above.
   Answer: D
   Jesus walked out behaviors that should have been familiar to believers at the time, but believers were not seeing them as familiar at all, even though they'd been reading and reading and reading the Scriptures. Jesus illustrated that standing around reading Scripture without living it out gets us disengaged from what it's actually saying. So, we should "rehash" it—read it, try it, talk about it—over and over and over. This is another reason

that we need the church body: to help motivate, inspire, and
edify (correct, teach) each other in God's Word.

9. **Church needs to be handled with one very specific attitude or
else it'll all go down the tubes. What is that attitude called?**

Agape love (the love that comes from God to us). This isn't
just churchy talk. Even an agnostic Harvard professor says
this about the church: "It's a world that's organized around a
particular mood, the mood of agape love. . . . It seems to me that
that mood wasn't really around until we had the community
that was organized around Jesus."[1]

■ Parent Primer #2: Little by Little . . .

From the beginning of time, humans have stumbled back into following rituals and rulers over God Himself. "I will not rule over you, nor will my son rule over you," Gideon told the begging Israelites back in the day. "The LORD will rule over you" (Judg. 8:23).

But the believers wanted a king, an earthly something they could cling to. "Appoint a king," they later said to the biblical prophet Samuel, "to lead us, such as all the other nations have" (1 Sam. 8:5).

As parents, we get this. Our kids rarely like anything dished out to them in a way that requires thought, reflection, discipline, input from the Holy Spirit, study, confidence, submission, and patience, which to kids sounds like blah, blah, blah, ugh. They'd prefer we spoon-feed them, which annoys them too, but at least they can tell when class is finished for the day.

If the first-century church is any indication, our kids come by their desire for packaged religion naturally. At first, early churches' vibrant, interactive get-togethers stood in stark contrast to other rituals of that time, like regularly scheduled Greco-Roman lectures modeled after Socrates. However, by the second and third centuries, spontaneous preaching by the "unschooled" (Acts 4:13) was giving way to a secular Greek tradition called a "homily," delivered by educated teachers before a passive crowd. Common attire gave way to elevated dress. Informality gave way to formality.

Not long into their faith walk, believers were told to "wake up!" (Rev. 3:2) and were prone to forsake their first love (God) (Rev. 2:4).

Believers rallied and, over the years, fought for the faith. One Roman ruler after another tried to snuff out Christians, like the emperor Nero, who burned, bludgeoned, and tortured Christians. He also blamed Christians for starting the Great Roman Fire of AD 64, alleging they'd done it to fulfill their prophecy that Rome would be destroyed by fire.[2]

As we mentioned in part 1, Christian believers found desperate relief when Constantine the Great issued the Edict of Milan, which mandated tolerance for Christianity some three hundred years after Christ rose from the dead. But relief came with compromises.

Constantine's reign was a season that popularized and politicized the church. Folks who wanted political or business favors could score points with Constantine if they adopted Christianity. It meant membership growth, but not necessarily spiritual growth for the actual members.[3]

Little by Little . . .

You've heard about politics in school, politics in the news, politics that have people sounding rather mean and nasty and as though the issues at hand are hopeless. Well, the church went through a time like that way back at the beginning. First, Christians were tortured for believing in Jesus. Then when they started to get relief from that horror, politics crept in. Some people began to fake what they believed so they'd get in good with the people in power. Let's talk about that, but let the record show that as for us and this house, we do not feel responsible to fake anything in our faith. The church body is a huge blessing, but don't let its structure get you feeling like you have to fake things to fit in.

1. **True or False: People do not try to fit in; people are independent thinkers who think for themselves in critical, methodical ways, no matter how it might help or hurt them in a group.**
   A. True. Often people do have thoughts and opinions that they hold in high regard.
   B. False. People may hold their thoughts in high regard, but they also want community. It's good to allow other voices of reason to influence us.
   C. True-ish and false-ish. People have opinions, people like community, and also people like power. So, they sometimes squash their own will or fake their feelings so they fit in with whoever has the most power.
   D. All of the above.
   Answer: D
   By the way, nobody admits it. That's another reason we need the church. There is nothing, nothing, nothing better than a friend who calls us out on

our true-ish, false-ish power-grab life moments, when we fake a feeling just to fit in with the power crowd. That sort of thing is very hard to pick up on in ourselves.

2. **Did believers rebel against God's ideas all along the Bible's story line? Like, no thanks, God, we want to go our own way?**

On and off, yes. They would ditch God's teaching on how they should run their lives and instead seek out tangible structures like everybody else around them had. Here are examples:

- Back in the day, God was supposed to rule the Israelites, but they came to Gideon instead. But Gideon said, "I will not rule over you, nor will my son rule over you. The LORD will rule over you" (Judg. 8:23).
- But the believers wanted a king, an earthly something they could cling to. "Appoint a king," they later said to the early biblical prophet Samuel, "to lead us, such as all the other nations have" (1 Sam. 8:5).

3. **Why do we care about that question above? It's not even about church and aren't we talking about the church?**

We care about that question because it addresses the fact that people are geared toward rituals and rulers that are a little more "packaged" than God. Like we said a few pages ago, God likes people to know him but not like he's a to-do list. It's actually rather hard to stick with God's idea on that because it requires structure (but not too legal-like) and also flexibility (but not too loose).

It's nice to know that at least this is nothing new. Our ancestors struggled with the same temptation.

4. **Did the early church do everything perfectly?**

No. In fact, some church members were told they needed to "wake up!" (Rev. 3:2).

They were also in trouble for forsaking their first love (God) (Rev. 2:4).

The church has never been perfect. Good thing for us, because we are not perfect, so we'll fit right in.

5. **What did infamous Roman emperor Nero have to say about Christians from the early church?**
   A. "I love them!"
   B. "Rome is burning and those Christians did it! Kill them!"
   C. "I don't care what they believe so long as they pay taxes."
   Answer: B
   For the first few hundred years of Christianity, one Roman ruler after another tried to snuff out Christians, like the emperor Nero, who burned, bludgeoned, and tortured Christians. He also blamed Christians for starting the Great Roman Fire of AD 64. He said Christians did it so Christians could claim that they were right about a prediction they made that Rome would be destroyed by fire. (P.S. Nero made that up. He was *mean*.)[4]

6. **Why did Constantine the Great say, "Everybody be nice to the Christian church!" in the second century?**
   A. He had a momentous conversion in battle and became a Christian.
   B. His wife told him to.
   C. His friends were becoming Christian and he wanted to fit in.
   Answer: A[5]

7. **The early believers were spreading the "gospel." We know gospel means "good news" but what do people *mean* when they say that?**
   • When God made the universe, he gave humans authority over the earth. However, humans wanted to be on the same level as the Creator of the earth. This made a break between God and humans. (See Adam, Eve, snake, fruit, tree, and several regrettable decisions.)
   • The only way God could solve this would be through a human. Why? Because it was humans who broke the

relationship, so it was a human who would have to repair the relationship.

- But no human on their own could do that. So God was willing to clothe himself in human flesh and do it himself. (Hello, Jesus.)
- Jesus absorbed the broken relationship (called sin) into his own earthly body when he willingly went to the cross. Then, because he had jurisdiction over his own body (John 10:18), he rose from the dead. In doing this, Jesus crushed the power of death (evil), which is a little hard to explain but is very, very real.
- Since evil wasn't the boss of Jesus, we get to claim that same thing. Bad things still happen, but evil does not have the last word in our lives; Jesus does, if we let him.
- When we submit to the fact that Jesus did this for us, we experience God overcoming any current and future brokenness we have with God, which means we get to be with God now and forever. We receive the Holy Spirit and he instructs us on how to run our race to help restore all parts of God's creation back into relationship with him. That is very, very good news!

CHAPTER 11

The Church's Breakups

■ Parent Primer #1: Hello, Denominations

WE WOULD LIKE to say that the church proceeded to mature and grow in unity. Instead, starting around the eleventh century, believers began breaking up with each other.

How exactly? In three wildly oversimplified steps, it goes like this:

1. Christians in western Europe considered the apostle Peter to be the first pope. They said Peter was the rock upon which Jesus built the church (Matt. 16:18) meaning Peter had jurisdiction over the entire church body and, therefore, so should the pope. However, Christians farther east said "on this rock" meant on the *faith* of Peter, not the *person* Peter, so having a central leader in power evermore was not the best idea. A lot more than that happened, but essentially, in 1054, splitsville. Church to the West was thereafter (Latin) Catholic; church to the East was thereafter (Greek) Orthodox.

2. A few centuries later a German monk named Martin Luther thought a friar named Johann Tetzel, at the behest of the pope, was running a shady fundraising scam. Tetzel was getting church congregants to pay money for prayers to get their deceased family members out of purgatory (a not-heaven-but-also-not-hell

component of Catholic theology).[1] Luther was saying the pope was wrong on this and other matters (a big no-no—you were not supposed to say the pope was wrong about anything back then), and Luther also denounced certain doctrines of Roman Catholicism. His ninety-five theses gave birth to the *solas*, meaning "alone," as in grace alone, faith alone, Christ alone, Scripture alone, glory to God alone. A lot more than that happened, but thus was Protestantism ushered in.

3. Around that same time, the Church of England broke up with Rome because Henry VIII wanted to start a new church because he couldn't get the pope to agree that ditching his first wife was fine. A lot more than that happened, but thus was ushered in Anglicanism.

As a result, all Christian churches today largely fall under these main categories: Catholic, Protestant, Orthodox, and Anglican (although, FYI, most people say Anglican *is* Protestant, but nevertheless, those are the big four).

Lots more breakups happened within those categories, forming groups like Lutheran, Presbyterian, Methodist, Baptist, and more. Reasons are innumerable, ranging from emphasis on the poor to heavier focus on evangelism to shunning hierarchy, like nineteenth-century preacher Charles Spurgeon (remember him from part 1?) who said clergy should not be ordained, so he refused and dodged the term "reverend."[2]

That said, some churches have come full circle from the ideologies that broke them up in the first place. "I am very encouraged by the discussions between the Catholics and the Lutherans where they came to an agreement, *Yes*, we affirm justification by grace through faith—imagine that!" said Asbury Theological Seminary's Ben Witherington. "In other words, we are *miles* from medieval Catholicism."[3]

Even so, most church gatherings today have some add-ons to their rituals or traditions that simply were not part of the first-century church. And really, why not?

Who knows whether the early apostles wouldn't appreciate the practicalities of official buildings instead of home churches, or weekly homilies delivered from a stage, or Communion crackers with a thimble of grape juice? Many of today's modern upgrades help believers know more, grow more, show more love.

We just cannot roll them out to the world under the guise of *sola scriptura*.

———————

Hello, Denominations

Okay, let's keep this intro short because today we're running through how the churches all broke up in the first place. We know you'll see all this explanation and think one thing: *NEVER MIND, please forget I ever asked*. But, it's interesting, and frankly, it's important to understand how we got where we are.

1. **Starting around the eleventh century, church members had big disagreements, and over time the church has been broken into four main branches.**
   - Roman Catholic.
   - Protestant.
   - Orthodox.
   - Anglican (FYI, most people say Anglican *is* Protestant, but nevertheless, those are the big four).

2. **What's a denomination?**
   It's a subset of one of the above branches.

3. **Why did these breakups come about? What happened?**
   This is the short, oversimplified version of what happened, but it kinda gives you the idea.
   Step One: Christians in western Europe considered the apostle Peter to be the first pope. They said Peter was the rock upon which Jesus built the church (Matt. 16:18), meaning Peter had jurisdiction over the entire church body and, therefore, so should the pope. However, Christians farther east said "on this rock" meant on the *faith* of Peter, not the *person* Peter, so having a central leader in power evermore was not the best idea. A lot more than that happened, but essentially, in 1054, splitsville.

Church to the West was thereafter (Latin) Catholic; church to the East was thereafter (Greek) Orthodox.

Step Two: A few centuries later a German monk named Martin Luther thought a friar named Johann Tetzel, on the orders of the pope, was running a shady fundraising scam. Tetzel was getting church congregants to pay money for prayers to get their deceased family members out of purgatory (a not-heaven-but-also-not-hell place in Catholic theology).[4] Luther was saying the pope was wrong on this and other matters (a big no-no—you were not supposed to say the pope was wrong about anything back then), and Luther also denounced certain doctrines of Roman Catholicism. His ninety-five theses gave birth to the *solas*, meaning, "alone," as in grace alone, faith alone, Christ alone, Scripture alone, glory to God alone. A lot more than that happened, but that's how Protestantism was ushered in.

Step Three: Around that same time, the Church of England broke up with Rome because Henry VIII wanted to start a new church because he couldn't get the pope to agree that ditching his first wife was fine. A lot more than that happened, but thus was ushered in Anglicanism.

4. **Why not just ignore the differences now and everybody join together?**
   A. We should! All those differences didn't mean anything then, and we should ignore them now.
   B. We should not! We couldn't possibly all pray the same, sing the same, worship the same.
   C. We might find that some of the differences are not going to work under the same roof for worship. Differences of opinion on things like Communion (everybody join in or just members?), baptism (adults? babies?), and evangelism (emphasis on converting people or clothing the poor?) present real differences.
   Answer: C

However, just so you know, some churches have gotten over big differences that broke them up in the first place. "I am very encouraged by the discussions between the Catholics and the Lutherans where they came to an agreement, *Yes*, we affirm justification by grace through faith—imagine that!" said Asbury Theological Seminary's Ben Witherington. "In other words, we are *miles* from medieval Catholicism."[5]

5. **Christians who make church choices for thought-out reasons should nonetheless remain fiercely kind and considerate to people from other churches. Why?**
   • Because if anyone can be different and yet united it should be the church (Eph. 1:10).
   • Because Jesus said, "By this everyone will know that you are my disciples, if you love one another" (John 13:34–35).

6. **What is one way we can hold one another accountable to show respect for *different* churches?**
   We can remind each other that the respect we show for different churches is a direct reflection of *our* church and how well it is teaching us to pay attention to our job as the church to highly value, care for, and demonstrate love for others (John 13:34; 1 Cor. 12:25–26).

■ Parent Primer #2: We Are Family

We parents get sweaty at the simple expectation to *be* the church body because the job is enormous. Not to mention we believers repeatedly get lots of things . . . *wrong.* We've been neglecting the alien, the orphan, and the widow since Jeremiah 7:6–8. Actually, we started that bad behavior in Isaiah 1:17. In fact, if we're getting honest, we'd have to throw it back all the way to Deuteronomy 10:17–19: "For the LORD your God is God of gods and Lord of lords, the great God, mighty and awesome, who . . . defends the cause of the fatherless and the widow, and loves the foreigner residing among you, giving them food and clothing. And you are to love those who are foreigners, for you yourselves were foreigners in Egypt."

Alas, dearest Father . . . don't count on it.

All that, plus our witness to Jesus's ministry? His resurrection? The good news?

Repeatedly not great.

We believers still cower at the worst times, like Peter who, when questioned about whether he knew Jesus, cursed just to drive home the lie that *no he did not* (Mark 14:66–72). Then after his profound experience with the Holy Spirit, Peter still decided to dodge new believers when his old church buddies were coming to town (Gal. 2:11–13).

That kind of behavior sounds all too familiar to us.

Why, why, *why* has the God of the Bible entrusted the people of the Bible and believers today with being his "co-workers in God's service . . . God's field, God's building" (1 Cor. 3:9)?

If the church is Christ's bride, then getting church "right" will take about as long as the phrase, "Now and as long as we both shall live."

We *have* had some brothers and sisters who rose up as shiny examples for us all, and they are worth mentioning here. There's Corrie ten Boom (whom we talked about in previous chapters) and her Christian counterparts, who suffered in Nazi prison camps for systematically hiding their Jewish neighbors from the Germans in World War II. There's Desmond Tutu, who used his Jesus-loving

ideals to restrain, resolve, and ultimately end South African apartheid. There's Congolese gynecologist Denis Mukwege, who has dedicated his career to caring for rape victims in the Democratic Republic
of Congo and was awarded the 2018 Nobel Peace Prize.[6]

Then there's the random man on that random city street cor-
ner who handed a twenty-two-year-old agnostic a copy of the New
Testament with Proverbs and Psalms. That agnostic, who happened
to be the now-famous comedian and host of *The Late Show* Stephen
Colbert, opened the Bible's frozen pages, read from the gospel of
Matthew, and—just like that—changed his agnostic mind.

"I had lost my faith in God, to my own great grief," said Colbert to
the Rev. James Martin on an episode of the Reverend's talk show. "I
was sort of convinced that I had been wrong all this time, that I had
been taught something that wasn't true."[7]

Until one of us, one small part of a centuries-strong global church,
made himself available in a simple way, handing out Bibles on a cold
street corner.

Then God took it from there.

Colbert said, "For the first time, I understood the real meaning of
the phrase, 'it spoke to me.' Like it read off the page. Like the words
of Christ just read off the page. It was no effort. And I stood on that
street corner in the cold and read the sermon. And my life has never
been the same."

This, we parents must effectively convey to our kids: God does not
show himself through his church because we are good at what we do
or even because we do what he says. He shows himself through relationship with his *family*.

Believers are not the princes or chiefs or builders of cities or rulers
of kingdoms, as we see in the genealogies of Cain. No, we are sons
and daughters, mothers and fathers, as denoted in the genealogy of
Seth to Shem to Abraham to Ruth to David to Jesus.

We are a family, and families live out their love through relationships, which sometimes look good and sometimes look bad, and that
reveals who they are.

We are a family that cannot do without God. It is an equation: we, without God, are . . . without. We cannot do life without God; we cannot do death without God.

This is being the church. Receiving the power of the Holy Spirit, acting when God says act, recalibrating and reshaping as we go, and when God shows himself, standing at the ready with edifying language. The point is, God's idea is to live out life with us as a family, and it is in seeing that that the world sees him. That's why we needn't be perfect, we need only be in relationship with him.

Some denominations call it salvation, then sanctification; others call it born again, then walking out our faith walk. Whatever the denominational lingo, we believers understand the gravity of Jesus's gift. We know that our utter vulnerability, our nakedness from the garden since the beginning of time, has been thwarted by Jesus's resurrection. We understand what we've been rescued from.

Still, we need daily recalibrating and reshaping. And we want desperately for our kids to take their place and do their part in that body of believers.

It's not fancy. It's family.

We Are Family

After reading about all the church breakups, did it cross your mind that when it comes to being the body of Christ, we are not that great at it? Like, all the way over to pretty average-to-partly-cloudy? As in, is the body of believers even the best crew for what God is hoping to accomplish?

By the way, do you even know what God wants to accomplish through the church? Here it is: he wants to show himself to the world. He wants to show himself to you. He wants his created humans to *know* him as Creator and Savior and Lord. He demonstrates himself directly through the Holy Spirit. He demonstrates himself through his Word. And also, he demonstrates himself through his relationship with his church (that's us).

Let's talk about why he thinks that's such a good idea.

1. **Why has the God of the Bible entrusted the people of the Bible and believers today with being his "co-workers in God's service . . . God's field, God's building" (1 Cor. 3:9)?**
   A. That's so obvious: because we're awesome.
   B. That's so obvious: because we're a family. In seeing that relationship play out, the world sees him.
   C. That's so obvious: we do everything he says.
   Answer: B
   Believers are not the princes or chiefs or builders of cities or rulers of kingdoms, as we see in other parts of the Bible. No, we are sons and daughters, mothers and fathers, like those listed in the genealogy of Seth to Shem to Abraham to Ruth to David to Jesus. The point is, God's idea is to live out life, with us, as a family, and it is in seeing that that the world sees him. That's why we needn't be perfect, we need only be in relationship with him.

2. **If God cannot show himself through our perfection (since we're not perfect), what does he show himself through?**
   - Our updating.
   - Our reshaping.
   - Our receiving the power of the Holy Spirit.

   This is being the church. Acting when God says act, updating and reshaping as we go, and when God shows himself, standing at the ready to tell God's story. It's not fancy. It's family.

3. **How exactly do we, as the church, show Christ to the rest of the world?**
   A. Stand up for justice, like Corrie ten Boom when she hid Jewish neighbors.
   B. Use our jobs to serve people in need, like Congolese gynecologist Denis Mukwege, who has dedicated his career to caring for girls in the Democratic Republic of Congo who have been assaulted and hurt in unimaginable ways. He was awarded the 2018 Nobel Peace Prize.[8]
   C. Take our Jesus-loving ideals to the highest political levels, like Desmond Tutu, who ultimately ended South African apartheid.
   D. Stand on a street corner and hand out Bibles on a freezing cold day.
   E. All of the above.

   Answer: E

   All of the above and more. Just remember, lots of our ancestors tried to "showcase" God and wound up not showcasing God. They wound up really disappointing themselves when they wanted to wow the crowd with "Look how great God is!"[9]

   So don't feel like you need to do something big. Start with this: act like someone who has love to spare, not someone who has a God to showcase.

   Know that God is already pursuing the people around you (2 Peter 3:9). They'll be looking at you to see if how the Holy

Spirit is nudging them is actually something they can act on in real-world ways.

Act like someone who is deeply, thoroughly loved by God. Because we are.

4. What if we are not ready or undereducated or simply terrified to do most of those things listed in the last question?

We should just do the next small step that's right in front of our faces. Any of us may be called to do some big job, but the most important thing every one of us can do is whatever is right there within our reach. Then we do it again the next day and again the next. It is in the small but consistent acts of affection and responsibility that families are held together, strengthened, and driven forward in purpose and growth. That's true of our walk as the church body as well.

5. And after we have done that small step day after day, what comes next?

That's up to God. That's what makes this community different than a club membership.

Here's how that played out for a now-famous comedian, Stephen Colbert, after a random guy handed him a little Bible while standing on a street corner: Colbert said, "For the first time, I understood the real meaning of the phrase, 'it spoke to me.' Like it read off the page. Like the words of Christ just read off the page. It was no effort. And I stood on that street corner in the cold and read the sermon. And my life has never been the same."[10]

Nothing, nothing, nothing that guy on the corner could have done except handing him the Bible would have made Colbert have that exact reaction to what he read.

We, the body of Christ, do not possess the perfect formula to bring about a predictable result. We have a relationship with God. We do what is ours to do. We watch God do what is his.

And he will.

CHAPTER 12

The Church's Future

■ Parent Primer #1: Practice Believing

THERE ARE KINDLY, friendly types of people in the world who do not believe in God and who want to save our kids the embarrassment of buying off on something that is not real.

Interestingly enough, so do we.

God is real. It's on us, the adults in the church body, to practice believing in practical ways so that our kids can see firsthand that we are not trying to sell them on pixie dust. Neither are we on the hook to demonstrate God's "GOD-ness" to them. That's on God. Our job is to let his truth speak for itself even while we speak it aloud to our kids.

One cutting-corners way that we parents can accidentally promote pixie dust rather than educating our kids on the real God is to privilege one of God's truths over another. An example?

Privileging the idea of faith (Ps. 46:10) over action (Gal. 2:10) or vice versa.

Rev. Tim Keller hit on this notion during a 2004 sermon. "Does the Spirit of God save souls? Yes," he told his New York congregation. "God does save souls, but he also takes enormous delight in growing and cultivating and enriching and caring for the well-being of his creation" (Ps. 104:30).[1]

We are to be the hands and feet through which he does that.

Bible hero David balanced these concepts well when facing Goliath. David had a unique clarity that even though it was God's power that downed the giant, it was still on David to pick up his rocks and run at Goliath. In fact, David had to make several purposeful choices along the way, like rejecting his brother's heckling (1 Sam. 17:28–31), rejecting Saul's offer of big armor (vv. 38–39), and getting up on that hill at all.

That kind of action does not attempt to orchestrate God's promises outside of God. It does, however, ground our faith in real life.

Understanding where we fit in God's plans does not always have clear demarcations. It would be easier, dare we say, if the system were a little more . . . either/or. As in *either* we count on God *or* we count on ourselves. That we can handle.

But God's system of "renewing the face of the earth" is set up such that we are to count on God to be God and count on ourselves to, well, be ourselves, whatever that means in any given situation.

If we're honest, better discernment on this matter might have helped the church avoid temper-tantrum behaviors over the past few centuries. For posterity, we should name a few, so our kids hear it from us first.

Like Puritan Oliver Cromwell's killing and crushing in the name of his political regime's form of "church," which exacted a brutal slaughter of Catholics.[2] (This was also in the name of legitimizing Henry VIII's wont to blow off one wife for another, so, you know, double bad.)

There's also the church-sanctioned idea of "divine right of kings" that legalized, formalized, and functionalized folks like Louis XIV and Marie Antoinette to let peasants starve to death while saying (in the now-famous if inaccurate quote), "Let them eat cake!"[3]

There are the secret political societies, like the upper class "Know Nothings" from the late 1800s, who made sure only folks from their church affiliation were voted into any local, city, or state government positions of power, ever. When asked about it, they replied, "We know nothing about that."[4]

Unfortunately, all these wrongheaded ideas about church have confused how faith in action is actually supposed to look. It has contributed to modern comments made about the church like this one: "At some point, there is going to be enough pressure that it is just going to be too embarrassing to believe in God," said neuroscientist and leading "new atheist" Sam Harris.[5]

We parents want our kids to stand on the other side of comments like that and experience one thing: certainty of what they believe. Not necessarily certainty of what they should say (even though we have 1 Peter 3:15 breathing down our necks) but certainty of what they believe.

For that to happen, our kids depend on the church body to articulate what's real about God and to let God's light shine, rather than package him or pamphlet him or privilege one of his truths over another.

"Christianity in the United States hasn't done a good job of engaging serious Christian reflection," said L. Gregory Jones, a senior strategist for leadership and education at Duke University.[6]

We can change that. As we do, our church body will grow stronger and our kids will grow in their gut-level certainty and intellectual foundation that we are not trafficking in religion here. We are dealing in relationship with God. One who is real.

———

Practice Believing

We've said this for years, but maybe we need to say it again, more directly: God is real. We talk about faith and pray about our lives and read the Bible for one reason: God is real. And we know he's real because we see him doing things in our lives and other people's lives.

Does that sound obvious to you? Have you known that all this time?

Because if we're getting honest here, it's an idea that comes and goes for Bible characters. They slip in and out of behavior that looks more like religion than relationship with a real God, and it gets them in trouble every time.

So, just to remind you, we're not members of a club. There's no time clock to punch so that you stay up on your fees. The body of Christ is not a social crew meant to get us on track to be nicer or more moral or better community members or kinder to our siblings or friends or parents. All that is an amazing by-product, but our reason for membership in the body of Christ is we are a group of people who simply believe God actually is who he says he is.

The activity of the church body after that is living life like God is real. Let's discuss that because believe us when we say it is weirdly way harder to do than you might think.

1. **Life isn't easy, sure, but remembering the simple fact that God is real seems like it should be easy, right?**

   It isn't easy for everyone. If it isn't easy for you, you're not alone.

   Public personalities will throw down the gauntlet and challenge the church like this: "At some point, there is going to be enough pressure that it is just going to be too *embarrassing* to believe in

God."[7] Standing steady in these cases can be a lot of things, but *easy* is not one of them.

Christians have been known to slide into a false sense of security that gets us behaving like maniacs just to prove a point or secure an edge over nonbelievers. That is not living like God is real. The church greatly needs to hold one another accountable on this point. It has not been easy, as past church history shows.

2. **Doesn't 1 Peter 3:15 say we should be ready with an answer for our faith if someone asks? Therefore shouldn't we have an answer at the ready if someone speaks like that guy did about God?**

We should be clear about what we believe, but that verse is not an order to have a quip and comeback every time someone offends God.

3. **What's so bad about the church having a quip and comeback every time someone offends God?**

That attitude can distract us from tracking with God and instead get us defending a religion, which leads to us excusing bad behavior, like the following:

- Puritan Oliver Cromwell's killing and crushing in the name of his political regime's "church," which exacted a brutal slaughter of Roman Catholics.[8] (This was also in the name of legitimizing Henry VIII's habit of blowing off one wife for another, so, you know, double bad.)
- There's also the church-sanctioned idea of "divine right of kings" that made it okay for folks like Louis XIV and Marie Antoinette to let peasants starve to death while saying, (in the now-famous if inaccurate quote), "Let them eat cake!"[9]
- There are the secret political societies, like the upper class "Know Nothings" from the late 1800s, who made sure only folks from their church affiliation were voted into any local, city, or state government positions of power, ever. When asked about it, they replied, "We know nothing about that."[10]

4. **Those examples happened a long time ago. Hasn't the church gotten a lot better at showing ourselves as consistent, caring, critical thinkers?**

It is reasonable to assume that the people reportedly leaving church today are not telling their friends over coffee, "I had to get out of that place because churchgoers are so *consistent*. They deal with real life openly and honestly and just know God will show himself through that." And that, unfortunately, shows that the church still has work to do.

5. **What can be done about this? How do we get better at living out our love of God with consistency, in a caring way, while thinking carefully about how we think and act?**

A. Practice. As we discussed a few chapters ago, we can invoke the Kathy Keller strategy—"Practice, practice, practice. Trial and error, repetition,"[11]—in all areas of the church and simply live out believing in God, one small step at a time.

B. Avoid. We can avoid trying to score members to join our church club by overpackaging God. The Bible is longer than a pamphlet for a reason. Not that nice marketing is a problem, but we have to put in the work to build our gut-level certainty and intellectual understanding that God is real.

C. Both of the above.

Answer: C

Also, neither of these is a one-hit wonder. We'll strengthen the body of Christ if we do these things over and over, build them into habits, and hold one another accountable when we're veering off track from them.

6. **Why are we talking so much about all this? We believe God, and we go to heaven. That's the bulk of it, right?**

Here's a pastor quote that might address that. "Does the Spirit of God save souls? Yes," Rev. Tim Keller told a New York congregation. "God does save souls, but he also takes enormous delight in growing and cultivating and enriching and caring for the well-being of his creation" (Ps. 104:30).[12] It's on us to be the hands and feet through which he does that.

7. **True or False: I thought being a Christian meant pressure's *off*. What we are discussing here sounds like pressure's *on*.**
   - *True.* This is not what we were sold when we were littler and we were told stories like David and Goliath, where David tossed a rock at a giant and bam! Thanks to God's intervention, just like that the world was better.
   - *False.* Even though it was God's power that helped David bam! the giant, David still had to pick up his rocks and run at Goliath. In fact, David had to make several purposeful choices along the way, like rejecting his brother's heckling (1 Sam. 17:28–31), rejecting Saul's offer of big armor (vv. 38–39), and getting up on that hill at all. "Pressure's off" is not the same thing as permission to be passive if that's not what God has intended.

   What we're discussing here is not *pressure's on*; what we are discussing are practical ways to be a contender, like we discussed in earlier chapters.

■ Parent Primer #2: Practice Power

In Bible language, this is what it looked like to practice raw, all-encompassing, dominating power: wrap a towel around your waist and wash the feet of those who don't understand things as you do (John 13:3–7). Then remind all those you love that this act does not diminish you, but rather this is what power looks like (John 13:13–16).

Harnessing that power means doing one small act after another, like Jesus did.

The church practicing its power would look like this: spreading the good news (Acts 2:18), stirring one another up to love and good deeds and encouragement (Heb. 10:24–25), and tending to the poor (Gal. 2:10).

The church has been known to do all of that and then, unfortunately, run out of steam. Of course we would. It is exhausting just reading that list above, much less keeping up with it day after month after year after millennium.

Which is to say, in the same way that we the body of Christ need to practice just about everything that makes up our faith, we need to practice employing the power that is ours in the Holy Spirit.

"The power which upstages the power of the Roman Empire is the power of love," says New Testament scholar N. T. Wright. "So much ancient religion, like so much modern religion, is about fear. It's about 'you gotta do this, otherwise the gods are coming to get you.' Some people try to do Christianity like that and it's completely wrong."[13]

Harnessing the power that the Holy Spirit bestows upon the church demands that we, the body of Christ, reject that type of fear and instead "get our act together," says Asbury Theological Seminary's Ben Witherington. "Unless the Church is . . . deliberately working out the unity we have in the spirit, then why should the world listen to us?"[14]

Our modern weekly gatherings have morphed into dramatically different-looking places than first-century churches, with hundreds, sometimes thousands, of members who may not even know one another.

We may not all have personal alliances with one another. We might not all even get along that well. Yet, "There is a spiritual unity in the body. All genuine Christians have a de facto unity that we simply need to recognize," says Witherington.[15]

We can choose to appreciate our big congregations and our small congregations, even if we do not agree on all things or run our gatherings the same way.

"We all have chinks in our armour," says Witherington,[16] but if we want the power that is ours in the Holy Spirit (and we do; we definitely, definitely do), it's on us as the church body to be Jesus to each other: to humbly wash one another's proverbial feet, valuing what each of us brings to the job of being the church.

We will find power in that unity, even if it is a body of believers that is under construction.

Practice Power

Do you know how many executive suites and workrooms and lecture halls and laboratories around the world are discussing, right now, how people can harness one kind of power or another? And God, the God who rescued us from separation from him, *has it all.* He has the power to write the laws of nature. He has the power to tell the ocean where to stop on the sand.

Do you know how he handles that power? He does not fly off to some nether place and puff out his chest, relishing his power. He comes to us. He rescues us. He invites us to participate in his plans.

Let's talk about that today.

1. **What is a great picture of how God handles his power?**

    Jesus wrapped a towel around his waist and washed the feet of those who didn't understand things as he did (John 13:3–7). And while he was doing it, he reminded all those he loved that this act did not diminish him, but it was instead a picture of what power looks like (John 13:13–16).

2. **Is this to suggest that the church body needs to more regularly wash each other's feet?**

    Not necessarily in a literal sense, but if we want the church to have the power that is ours in the Holy Spirit (and we do; we definitely, definitely do), it's on us as the church body to be feet-washers to each other.

    We church members can humbly wash one another's feet, so to speak, by helping one another and valuing what each of us brings to the job of being the church. In that unity, there is power. That doesn't mean we all have to be the same. In fact, the very fact that we are different means some are hands, and some are feet, like the Bible says (1 Cor. 12).

3. **What's one reason it is important for us to demonstrate the power of the body of Christ in this way?**
   There are lots of reasons, but one is that it's our best shot at the church having an influence over culture, rather than the other way around.[17]

4. **What is a key to not getting discouraged as believers, as the body of Christ, as the church?**
   A. "I ask you, therefore, not to be discouraged . . ." (Eph. 3:13).
   B. "That Christ may dwell in your hearts . . ." (Eph. 3:17).
   C. "That you, being rooted and established in love, may have power . . ." (Eph. 3:17–18).
   D. All of the above.
   Answer: D
   Yes, the answer is D, all of the above. We believers can carry on, able and well, knowing all, all, all of the above.

CONCLUSION

Before We Take Our Leave from One Another . . .

AFTER SLOGGING THROUGH lo these many pages, we parents can say one thing: possibility abounds.

The church has endless possibilities of community and support and edification. The Bible is possibly the greatest gift known to humankind. And prayer. Prayer harnesses for our children the infinite possibility of utter *un*aloneness.

Unfortunately, all these possibilities leave lots of wiggle room where parenting our kids in their faith could possibly go wrong. The weight of that is possibly going to make some of us bawl right now.

So before we take our leave from one another and these pages and this collective parental effort of honestly addressing our kids' hard faith questions, let us unite over one more brief story.

Once upon a time, an elementary school teacher emailed a little girl's mother to report that the little girl appeared to lack confidence. "She never raises her hand," the teacher said when the parent followed up with a phone call. "She's bright. I know she knows answers. But she does not volunteer in class."

The mother asked her daughter, privately, why she didn't raise her hand and speak in class.

The daughter offered her mother a withering look. "Mom. We get one recess all day," she said, as if that settled the matter. The parent looked blank until the child elaborated. "The teacher asks questions and kids raise their hands and I'm sitting there watching the clock the whole time and thinking *stop talking, stop talking, stop talking.*"

That daughter's confidence was fine.

Her goodwill, however, toward a system that kept her from running and playing? Not great.

To that end, the last thing we parents want to do is corner our kids into participating in another family chat that feels primarily like not-recess. Even worse, we parents do not want our kids to track what we're doing and then work the system—as in say what we want to hear so we all have time to play or so they feel like we approve or even so they feel like they belong.

We are a family. They already belong. They are our children. We already approve.

This is not an entrance exam to become a valued part of our family. This is us wanting them to actually know God. Deeply. In the way that will stick with them and direct them through the rest of their lives. Our longing for this cannot be overstated. If we thought that cornering them on the matter would work, then corner them we would. If we believed that setting them free would keep the conversation authentic as they grow, then we would do that all day and in every way.

We would move heaven and earth in order to download into them the correctly ascribed algorithm of Bible knowledge and practical information and personal experience and moral discipline and church doctrine that builds a deep and abiding relationship between them and God now and as long as we all shall live. Did we mention it is the most important agenda item on our parenting list?

The problem is, that kind of algorithm omits the Holy Spirit. The other problem is, there is no algorithm.

Stephen Colbert's mom is a great case in point. She had taught Colbert all about Jesus. The family had suffered gut-wrenching tragedy when a plane crash killed Colbert's dad and two brothers. Colbert testifies that his mother's faith is what sustained her and she modeled that to him. She had done all the things a parent should do, and yet her son, until one freezing day in Chicago, found that he just did not believe.

Ours is not to make our kids believe. Ours is to "train up a child in the way he should go: and when he is old, he will not depart from it" (Prov. 22:6 KJV).

There's such a fine line between doing that well versus obsessively waking in the middle of the night to jot ourselves a reminder: *schedule guy on street corner to meet son at age twenty-two. Bring Bible. Make it cold.* Yet if Colbert's story tells us anything, it's that we parents don't have control long before we even realize it.

We learn from our ancestors that our goal here is not about our kids sustaining a faith so much as it's about them receiving a faith that sustains them, a God who sustains them, a love that sustains them. Ours is simply to show them a life in faith and also to bolster their knowledge of him in ways that matter and resonate with this generation.

We so very much want to run this part of our race well.

Which is to say, things have not changed so very much. Parents love their kids. And yet "we know in part and we prophesy in part, but when completeness comes, what is in part disappears" (1 Cor. 13:9–10). All this work and we still, on our very best day, offer up to our kids only . . . part?

Yes.

We have just covered pages of data points and Bible points and interesting points to help us do one thing: carry on anyway. Together. As Christian parents for this generation, in the church body of Christ.

"Then he said to his disciples, 'The harvest is plentiful but the workers are few'" (Matt. 9:37).

We can believe that's true of our kids. They are a harvest of potential and plenty. We can celebrate this generation's inclination toward asking probing, exacting (albeit unnerving) questions about God and our faith's history and the everyday practicalities of our worldview and how it relates to friends and family and community and more.

They are the future of the body of Christ. We want our body strong. If that probing rattles us, shakes us, or unnerves us? Then we will hold steady while it does.

Let's fix our faces. Wipe off the panic. We are the workers and this is what the workers do. We walk in step with the Holy Spirit the best we can. We will know we have succeeded when . . . wait, how will we know we've succeeded? How does one measure our kids' relationship with Christ?

"I don't know that we can quantify that, and let me tell you why," said Asbury Theological Seminary's Ben Witherington. "Most real Christians' experience of God is much more profound than their understanding of God, never mind their ability to articulate what they understand of God."[1]

So, we parents of this generation give our kids the permission to flounder in their faith, even if it does not showcase us as perfect parents like we wish it would. God's given that permission to us for years, which works well for a God who is building a relationship, precept upon precept, and who seems rather optimistic that that way of us getting to know him is actually going to work.

It is less convenient for some of us parents who are white-knuckling this thing no matter what our fixed faces present.

Which circles us back to where we began. This is a new generation, and we can come at this situation with the help of words we maybe have not used in some time. *Dialegomai* is a fantastic one. An old word, yet we can use it fresh today as we steel our spines for talking out this stuff with our kids. It was good enough for Paul and for the apostles as they discussed, disputed, and reasoned in ways that spread around truths about what God is all about.

So we act now for these kids who are hitting ages in which they have questions they think we can answer and yet already have lives that we cannot live for them. We commit to standing with them as they dig, doubt, and dither if they have to—and we are here to *dialegomai* with them while they do.

"I will walk among you and be your God, and you will be my people. . . . I broke the bars of your yoke and enabled you to walk with heads held high" (Lev. 26:12–13).

Dearest heavenly Father, we, the parents of this generation, are counting on it.

DIGGING DEEPER

What Are the Dead Sea Scrolls?

THE DEAD SEA Scrolls are ancient manuscripts written between 250 BC and AD 70. In 1947 the first of eleven caves containing these long-hidden documents was found near Qumran (about twenty miles east of Jerusalem near the Dead Sea). The scrolls contain the oldest complete book of Isaiah, the Ten Commandments, and fragments from every other book in the Old Testament except the book of Esther.

These scrolls of the Old Testament are more than a thousand years older than any previous copies ever found. Amazingly, these ancient manuscripts are very close to the later ones and give us insight into how the Old Testament was passed on to us.[1]

Is There Evidence Outside the Bible for the Historical Jesus?

Yes, Roman and Jewish historians refer to Jesus Christ shortly after he lived and during the early spread of Christianity.

In his book *Jewish Antiquities*, Flavius Josephus (a Jewish historian who was not a Christian) mentions James, the "brother of Jesus who was called the Christ." He also refers to Jesus as "a wise man. . . . He was the achiever of extraordinary deeds and was a teacher. . . . He won over many Jews and many of the Greeks. . . . When he was indicted by the principal men among us and Pilate condemned him to be crucified, those who had come to love him originally did not cease to do so. . . . And the tribe of Christians, so named after him, has not disappeared to this day."[2]

A Roman historian, Tacitus, in his *Annals of Imperial Rome*, when writing about the burning of Rome during Nero's reign, writes disdainfully of Christians: "The founder of this name, Christ [Christus in Latin], had been executed in the reign of Tiberius by the procurator Pontius Pilate. . . . Suppressed for a time, the deadly superstition erupted again not only in Judea, the origin of this evil, but also in the city [Rome]."

A friend of Tacitus, Roman governor Pliny the Younger, wrote a letter to Emperor Trajan about Christians, who would "sing hymns to Christ as to a god."[3]

What Are the Main Genres in the Bible?

The biggest genre in the Bible is *narrative*, present in most of its books. This genre has plot, characters, themes, and generally a historical context. There is usually a chain of events that includes background information, some kind of conflict, rising action, climax, and resolution.

A second genre is *law*, like Leviticus and Deuteronomy. There are two main types of law codes: permanent prohibitions, like the Ten Commandments, and conditional prohibitions, or case law, which uses language like, "If this happens . . . then do this . . ." It's helpful to know that "the law" in the Scriptures comes from a Hebrew word meaning "instruction" or "to point the way." The Old Testament laws are instructions for how to live godly lives in right relationship with God and others.

A third genre is *poetry*, like the Psalms. Key features of poetry are vivid imagery, parallelism, repetition, and terseness. Unlike English poetry, rhyming does not play a role in biblical poetry. Songs, hymns, and some prophetic utterances have features of poetry.

A fourth genre is *wisdom*, predominantly seen in Proverbs, Job, and Ecclesiastes. These books contain practical guidelines and general principles for living moral and ethical lives.

A fifth genre is *prophecy*, like Isaiah. A key feature of prophecy is that it contains a warning followed by a judgment for disobedience, a promise for obedience, or both. Prophecy does not always tell what *will* happen. Rather, prophecy forthtells: it declares the current situation and God's assessment of it, includes a vision of possible outcomes for obedience or disobedience, gives a call to repentance, and intercedes for the people.

A sixth genre is *apocalyptic*, like parts of Daniel and Revelation. This genre has many of the same structural elements and features of the prophetic. However, it usually includes the introductory phrase "in that day," "the day is coming," or "it shall come to pass afterward," and specifies a particular event, place, and action, a declaration of what the Lord will do, and the result or consequence: "it will come to pass."

The last two genres are specific to the New Testament. The *Gospels* are mainly narrative, but they are also proclamation with eyewitness accounts of Jesus's life, teaching, death, resurrection, and ascension. Additional genres, such as parables, prophecy, poetry, and song are included in the Gospels.

The final genre is the *epistles*, or letters of the New Testament, written by various authors but primarily Paul. These are instructive but include historical accounts, hymns, poetry, and wisdom.

As you read through the Bible, see if you can identify different genres and if recognizing them helps you read and interpret them with better understanding.[4]

NOTES

Introduction

1. "Dialegomai," Blue Letter Bible, Strong's Concordance, accessed October 2, 2019, https://www.blueletterbible.org/lang/Lexicon /Lexicon.cfm?strongs=G1256&t=NASB. See also *A Greek-English Lexicon of the New Testament and Other Early Christian Literature*, 3rd ed., comp. Walter Bauer, ed. and rev. Frederick W. Danker (Chicago: University of Chicago Press, 2000), s.v. "διαλέγομαι."

Chapter 1: How the Bible Was Put Together

1. Elijah Hixon, "Was Spurgeon King James Only?," Spurgeon Center for Biblical Preaching at Midwest Seminary, January 18, 2018, https://www.spurgeon.org/resource-library/blog-entries /was-spurgeon-king-james-only.
2. Hixon, "Was Spurgeon King James Only?"
3. Jordan B. Peterson, "Biblical Series I: Introduction to the Idea of God," Jordan B Peterson, May 20, 2017, YouTube video, 2:38:28, https://youtu.be/f-wWBGo6a2w.
4. For more information on the old writings, see the Digging Deeper section "What Are the Dead Sea Scrolls?" on page 201.
5. Ryan M. Reeves and Charles E. Hill, *Know How We Got Our Bible* (Grand Rapids: Zondervan, 2018), 26.
6. Ben Witherington III, "Ben Witherington III: The Problem with Evangelical Theology," Unitas Fidei, April 25, 2016, YouTube video, 31:29, https://youtu.be/ndJd1XFihe8.
7. Milton Fisher, "The Canon of the New Testament," in *The Origin of the Bible*, ed. Philip Wesley Comfort, updated ed. (Wheaton, IL: Tyndale, 2003), 65–72.
8. David Brakke, "Canon Formation and Social Conflict in

Fourth-Century Egypt: Athanasius of Alexandria's Thirty-Ninth Festal Letter," *Harvard Theological Review* 87, no. 4 (October 1994): 395–419.

9. Jordan B. Peterson, "Tragedy vs Evil," Jordan B Peterson, March 30, 2013, YouTube video, 42:35, https://youtu.be/MLp7v WB0TeY.

10. Lynne Kelly, *Knowledge and Power in Pre-Historic Societies: Orality, Memory and the Transmission of Culture* (Cambridge: Cambridge University Press, 2015), 14–24. See also Robert D. Miller II, *Oral Tradition in Ancient Israel* (Eugene, OR: Cascade, 2011), 40–58.

11. Reeves and Hill, *Know How We Got Our Bible*, 83.

12. Reeves and Hill, *Know How We Got Our Bible*, 42. See also Paul Lawrence, "A Brief History of the Septuagint," Associates for Biblical Research, March 31, 2016, https://biblearchaeology.org /research/new-testament-era/4022-a-brief-history-of-the -septuagint.

13. Reeves and Hill, *Know How We Got Our Bible*, 87–88.

14. Ryan Reeves, "Early Christian Persecution," Ryan Reeves, May 27, 2014, YouTube video, 33:05, https://youtu.be/hJR0A9phBc8.

Chapter 2: The Bible's Reputation Among Scholars . . . and Us

1. Bart D. Ehrman, "The Gospels and the Existence of Jesus," *The Bart Ehrman Blog* (blog), October 27, 2016, https://ehrmanblog .org/the-gospels-and-the-existence-of-jesus/.

2. Bart D. Ehrman, "Did Jesus Exist?," *HuffPost*, March 20, 2012, https://www.huffpost.com/entry/did-jesus-exist_b_1349544.

3. N. T. Wright and Sean Kelly, "The Bible: Gospel, Guide, or Garbage?," December 12, 2013, in *Veritas Forum*, podcast, 1:32:04, http://www.veritas.org/the-bible-gospel-guide-or-garbage/.

4. Tim Keller and Anthony Kronman, "Disenchanted? Tim Keller & Anthony Kronman at Yale," March 30, 2017, in *Veritas Forum*, podcast, 1:18:54, http://www.veritas.org/disenchanted -tim-keller-anthony-kronman-yale/.

5. Keller and Kronman, "Disenchanted?"
6. Wright and Kelly, "The Bible: Gospel, Guide, or Garbage?"
7. Keller and Kronman, "Disenchanted?"
8. Josh McDowell and Sean McDowell, "Is the New Testament Historically Reliable?," in *Evidence That Demands a Verdict: Life-Changing Truth for a Skeptical World* (Nashville: Harper-Collins, 2017), chap. 3.

   See also Sheri Bell, "Testing the Historical Reliability of the New Testament," Josh McDowell Ministry, January 10, 2018, https://www.josh.org/historical-reliability-new-testament/; Sheri Bell, "Ancient Manuscripts That Validate the Bible's Old Testament," Josh McDowell Ministry, February 14, 2018, https://www.josh.org/manuscript-validate-old-testament/; and Matt Slick, "Manuscript Evidence for Superior New Testament Reliability," Christian Apologetics and Research Ministry, December 10, 2008, https://carm.org/manuscript-evidence.
9. Clay Jones, "The Bibliographical Test Updated," *Clay Jones* (blog), July 3, 2012, https://www.clayjones.net/2012/07/the-bibliographical-test-updated/.
10. Paul Copan, "Jesus' Followers Fabricated the Stories and Sayings of Jesus," Ravi Zacharias International Ministries, accessed October 2, 2019, https://www.rzim.org/read/just-thinking-magazine/jesus-followers-fabricated-the-stories-and-sayings-of-jesus.
11. Ehrman, "Did Jesus Exist?"
12. Wright and Kelly, "The Bible: Gospel, Guide, or Garbage?"
13. Elelwani B. Farisani, "Interpreting the Bible in the Context of Apartheid and Beyond: An African Perspective," *Studia Historiae Ecclesiasticae* 40, no. 2 (December 2014): 207–25.
14. Copan, "Jesus' Followers Fabricated the Stories."
15. Allan A. Boesak, "A Letter to the Minister of Justice," Abahlali baseMjondolo, August 24, 1979, http://abahlali.org/files/KAIROS_Boesak_Letter_personal%20declaration%20of%20faith.pdf.
16. Mark Noll, "Mark Noll: Race and Slavery in America's Bible

Civilization (3/31/2016)," wheatoncollege, April 7, 2016, You-Tube video, 1:18:13, https://youtu.be/unvPKqxJyc4.

17. Wright and Kelly, "The Bible: Gospel, Guide, or Garbage?"

18. Ehrman, "Did Jesus Exist?"

19. "You'll Be Back," featuring Jonathan Groff, by Lin-Manuel Miranda, recorded August 16–21, 2015, track 7 on *Hamilton*, Atlantic, 2015.

20. Wright and Kelly, "The Bible: Gospel, Guide, or Garbage?"

Chapter 3: Ancient Literature from Scripture Writers' Points of View

1. N. T. Wright, "N. T. Wright on the Eric Metaxas Radio Show," Eric Metaxas Radio Show, May 15, 2019, YouTube video, 1:03:23, https://youtu.be/5VXtIJ5wnyk.

2. John Walton, "The Lost World of Adam and Eve by Dr. John Walton," apologeticscom, June 2, 2015, YouTube video, 55:47, https://youtu.be/8fn1ESgtNi4.

3. "From the Dust: The Book of Genesis," BioLogos, January 15, 2012, 11:46, https://biologos.org/resources/from-the-dust-the -book-of-genesis.

4. "From the Dust," BioLogos.

5. Michael Halcomb and Ben Witherington III, "The Bible & Science: Dr. Michael Halcomb & Dr. Ben Witherington III," tmichaelwhalcomb, October 12, 2014, YouTube video, 51:58, https://youtu.be/tNv3ym57Qrs.

6. Don Carson, "How to Read the Bible and Do Theology Well," The Gospel Coalition, September 24, 2015, https://www.thegospel coalition.org/article/the-bible-and-theology-don-carson -nivzsb/.

7. Wayne Coppins, "Peter Arzt-Grabner on the Interpretation of IOYNIAN in Rom 16.7 (Paulus Handbuch Series)," *German for Neutestamentler* (blog), June 23, 2014, https://germanfor neutestamentler.com/2014/06/23/paulus-handbuch-peter-arzt -grabner-on-the-interpretation-of-ιουνιαν-in-rom-16-7/. See also N. T. Wright, "N.T. Wright on Women in Ministry 5," Steve

Yamaguchi, March 11, 2009, YouTube video, 4:41, https://youtu
.be/QaVVXleoAdU; and Marg Mowczko, "Junia in Romans
16:7," *Marg Mowczko* (blog), April 1, 2010, https://margmowczko
.com/junia-and-the-esv/.

Chapter 4: Outlining Unedited Prayer

1. Kathy Keller, "Flourishing Faith in Dangerous Places—Session
   3—Kathy Keller," City to City Australia, July 29, 2014, 44:17,
   https://vimeo.com/101991490.
2. Michael Halcomb and Ben Witherington III, "The Bible &
   Science: Dr. Michael Halcomb & Dr. Ben Witherington III,"
   tmichaelwhalcomb, October 12, 2014, YouTube video, 51:58,
   https://youtu.be/tNv3ym57Qrs.
3. Keller, "Flourishing Faith in Dangerous Places."
4. Keller, "Flourishing Faith in Dangerous Places."
5. Keller, "Flourishing Faith in Dangerous Places."
6. Keller, "Flourishing Faith in Dangerous Places."
7. Keller, "Flourishing Faith in Dangerous Places."
8. "Sarah," Blue Letter Bible, Strong's Concordance, accessed
   October 2, 2019, https://www.blueletterbible.org/lang/Lexicon
   /Lexicon.cfm?strongs=H8280&t=NASB. See also Ludwig Koehler and Walter Baumgartner, *The Hebrew and Aramaic Lexicon
   of the Old Testament*, vol. 4 (Leiden, Netherlands: Brill, 1999),
   1354.

Chapter 5: Sticking with Prayer Even When Circumstances Say Not To

1. Max Roser and Esteban Ortiz-Ospina, "Literacy," Our World in
   Data, September 20, 2018, https://ourworldindata.org/literacy.
2. "Decline of Global Extreme Poverty Continues but Has Slowed:
   World Bank," World Bank, September 19, 2018, https://www
   .worldbank.org/en/news/press-release/2018/09/19/decline-of
   -global-extreme-poverty-continues-but-has-slowed-world-bank.
3. Martijn Lampert and Anne Blanksma Çeta, "Towards 2030
   Without Poverty," Glocalities, accessed October 2, 2019, https://

www.glocalities.com/reports/towards-2030-without-poverty
?chronoform=Whitepaper-Poverty&event=submit.

4. Laura Miller, "David Foster Wallace," *Salon*, March 9, 1996, https://www.salon.com/1996/03/09/wallace_5/.

5. Antonis Katsiyannis, Denise K. Whitford, and Robin Parks Ennis, "Historical Examination of United States Intentional Mass School Shootings in the 20th and 21st Centuries: Implications for Students, Schools, and Society," *Journal of Child and Family Studies* 27, no. 8 (July 2018): 2562–73.

6. Mohsen Naghavi, "Global, Regional, and National Burden of Suicide Mortality 1990 to 2016: Systematic Analysis for the Global Burden of Disease Study 2016," *British Medical Journal* 364, no. 194 (2019): 1–11, https://www.bmj.com/content/364/bmj.l94.

7. Obituaries, "David Foster Wallace," *Telegraph*, September 15, 2008, https://www.telegraph.co.uk/news/obituaries/2965284/David-Foster-Wallace.html.

8. Meg Jay, *The Defining Decade: Why Your Twenties Matter and How to Make the Most of Them Now* (New York: Twelve, 2012), 22.

9. Jordan B. Peterson, "Reality and the Sacred," January 2, 2017, in *Jordan B. Peterson Podcast*, podcast, 58:18, https://www.jordanbpeterson.com/podcast/episode-1/.

10. Peterson, "Reality and the Sacred."

11. Corrie ten Boom with Elizabeth Sherrill and John Sherrill, *The Hiding Place*, 35th anniversary ed. (Grand Rapids: Chosen Books, 2006).

12. Ten Boom, *The Hiding Place*, 35th anniversary ed., 195.

13. Ten Boom, *The Hiding Place*, 35th anniversary ed., 195.

14. Corrie ten Boom with John Sherrill and Elizabeth Sherrill, *The Hiding Place: The Triumphant True Story of Corrie ten Boom*, reissue ed. (New Jersey: Bantam, 1974), 98–99.

15. Ten Boom, *The Hiding Place*, reissue ed., 50–53.

16. Ten Boom, *The Hiding Place*, reissue ed., 110–11.

17. Ten Boom, *The Hiding Place*, 35th anniversary ed., 195.

18. Ten Boom, *The Hiding Place*, 35th anniversary ed., 195.

Chapter 6: Picking God and Sticking with Him

1. Timothy J. Keller, "Abraham and the Torch," Gospel in Life, November 3, 1996, 28:28, https://gospelinlife.com/downloads /abraham-and-the-torch-5860/.

Part 3: Introduction for Parents

1. Ludwig Koehler and Walter Baumgartner, "Raqia`," in *The Hebrew and Aramaic Lexicon of the Old Testament*, vol. 4 (Leiden, Netherlands: Brill, 1999), 1290.
2. Wyatt Houtz, "John Calvin on Nicolaus Copernicus and Heliocentrism," BioLogos, October 28, 2014, https://biologos .org/articles/john-calvin-on-nicolaus-copernicus-and-helio centrism.
3. Augustine of Hippo, *St. Augustine: The Literal Meaning of Genesis*, vol. 1, Ancient Christian Writers, trans. and ed. Johannes Quasten, Walter J. Burghardt, and Thomas Comerford Lawler (Mahwah, NJ: Paulist Press, 1982), 41.

Chapter 7: Why Science and Faith Fight

1. Emily Dickinson, "Tell All the Truth but Tell It Slant— (1263)," Poetry Foundation, accessed October 2, 2019, https:// www.poetryfoundation.org/poems/56824/tell-all-the-truth -but-tell-it-slant-1263.
2. *Encyclopedia Britannica Online*, s.v. "Heliocentrism," accessed October 2, 2019, https://www.britannica.com/science/helio centric-system.
3. Gary DeMar, "Martin Luther and Copernicus," American Vision, December 18, 2006, http://americanvision.org/1264 /martin-luther-copernicus/.
4. Wyatt Houtz, "John Calvin on Nicolaus Copernicus and Heliocentrism," BioLogos, October 28, 2014, https://biologos .org/articles/john-calvin-on-nicolaus-copernicus-and-helio centrism.
5. John Warwick Montgomery, *In Defense of Martin Luther*, 2nd ed. (Irvine: NRP, 2017), 91.

6. Alvin J. Schmidt, *How Christianity Changed the World* (Grand Rapids: Zondervan, 2004), 226–27.

7. Keith Mathison, "Introduction—A Reformed Approach to Science and Scripture," Ligonier Ministries, May 4, 2012, https://www.ligonier.org/blog/introduction-reformed-approach-science-and-scripture/.

8. Alan Cowell, "After 350 Years, Vatican Says Galileo Was Right: It Moves," *New York Times*, October 31, 1992, https://www.nytimes.com/1992/10/31/world/after-350-years-vatican-says-galileo-was-right-it-moves.html.

9. Cowell, "After 350 Years, Vatican Says Galileo Was Right."

10. Bernard Ramm, *The Christian View of Science and Scripture* (Grand Rapids: Eerdmans, 1956), 17.

11. Ramm, *The Christian View of Science and Scripture*, 19–20.

12. Ramm, *The Christian View of Science and Scripture*, 19.

13. "From the Dust: The Book of Genesis," BioLogos, January 15, 2012, 11:46, https://biologos.org/resources/from-the-dust-the-book-of-genesis.

14. "From the Dust," BioLogos.

15. Augustine of Hippo, *St. Augustine: The Literal Meaning of Genesis*, vol. 1, Ancient Christian Writers, trans. and ed. Johannes Quasten, Walter J. Burghardt, and Thomas Comerford Lawler (Mahwah, NJ: Paulist Press, 1982), 41.

16. Cowell, "After 350 Years, Vatican Says Galileo Was Right."

17. Montgomery, *In Defense of Martin Luther*, 91.

18. Schmidt, *How Christianity Changed the World*, 226–27.

19. Mark Noll, "Scandal of the Evangelical Mind: An Interview with Mark Noll," Gordon College, November 6, 2009, YouTube video, 44:08, https://youtu.be/eQviXavl1BA.

20. Onnesha Roychoudhuri, "Our Rosy Future, According to Freeman Dyson," *Salon*, September 29, 2007, https://www.salon.com/2007/09/29/freeman_dyson/.

21. Gary Wolf, "The Church of the Non-Believers," *Wired*, November 1, 2006, https://www.wired.com/2006/11/atheism/.

22. Thalia Wheatley and Jonathan Haidt, "Hypnotic Disgust Makes

Moral Judgments More Severe," *Psychological Science* 16, no. 10 (2005): 780–84, https://bscw.rediris.es/pub/bscw.cgi/d4450466 /Wheatley-Hypnotic_disgut_makes_moral_judgments_more _severe.pdf.

23. Noll, "Scandal of the Evangelical Mind."
24. Roychoudhuri, "Our Rosy Future."
25. Wolf, "The Church of the Non-Believers."
26. Houtz, "John Calvin on Nicolaus Copernicus and Heliocentrism."

Chapter 8: Dissension Within Both Ranks

1. Steven Weinberg, "Steven Weinberg Discussion (3/8)—Richard Dawkins," Richard Dawkins Foundation for Reason & Science, July 15, 2008, YouTube video, 9:49, https://youtu.be/kNpiX8X QhJM.
2. Allan Silverman, "Plato's Middle Period Metaphysics and Epistemology," Stanford Encyclopedia of Philosophy, July 14, 2014, https://plato.stanford.edu/entries/plato-metaphysics/.
3. Steven Weinberg, "Steven Weinberg Discussion (2/8)—Richard Dawkins," Richard Dawkins Foundation for Reason & Science, July 15, 2008, YouTube video, 9:54, https://youtu.be/U2IisaN C4bE.
4. Antony Flew with Roy Abraham Varghese, *There Is a God: How the World's Most Notorious Atheist Changed His Mind* (San Francisco: HarperOne, 2008), 1.
5. Flew with Varghese, *There Is a God*, vii.
6. Flew with Varghese, *There Is a God*, 88.
7. Flew with Varghese, *There Is a God*, 88.
8. Tim Keller and Anthony Kronman, "Disenchanted? Tim Keller & Anthony Kronman at Yale," March 30, 2017, in *Veritas Forum*, podcast, 1:18:54, http://www.veritas.org/disenchanted -tim-keller-anthony-kronman-yale/.
9. Keller and Kronman, "Disenchanted?"
10. Weinberg, "Steven Weinberg Discussion (2/8)—Richard Dawkins."

11. Silverman, "Plato's Middle Period Metaphysics."
12. Silverman, "Plato's Middle Period Metaphysics."
13. Flew with Varghese, *There Is a God*, 88.
14. Flew with Varghese, *There Is a God*, 88.
15. Keller and Kronman, "Disenchanted?"
16. "New Genome Comparison Finds Chimps, Humans Very Similar at the DNA Level," National Human Genome Research Institute, March 12, 2012, https://www.genome .gov/15515096/2005-release-new-genome-comparison-finds -chimps-humans-very-similar-at-dna-level.
17. Michael Halcomb and Ben Witherington III, "The Bible & Science: Dr. Michael Halcomb & Dr. Ben Witherington III," tmichaelwhalcomb, October 12, 2014, YouTube video, 51:58, https://youtu.be/tNv3ym57Qrs.
18. Ryan Reeves, "Wesley and Whitefield," Ryan Reeves, July 1, 2015, YouTube video, 32:43, https://youtu.be/rgqicv3nRdg.
19. Mark Noll, foreword to *Think: The Life of the Mind and the Love of God*, by John Piper (Wheaton, IL: Crossway, 2010), 11–13.
20. Noll, foreword to *Think*, 13.
21. Halcomb and Witherington, "The Bible & Science."
22. "New Genome Comparison," National Human Genome Research Institute.
23. Francis S. Collins, "Why I'm a Man of Science—and Faith," *National Geographic*, March 19, 2015, https://news.nationalgeo graphic.com/2015/03/150319-three-questions-francis-collins -nih-science/.
24. Noll, foreword to *Think*, 11–13.

Chapter 9: Motivation Is Key

1. Ludwig Koehler and Walter Baumgartner, "Raqia`," in *The Hebrew and Aramaic Lexicon of the Old Testament*, vol. 4 (Leiden, Netherlands: Brill, 1999), 1290.
2. Alister McGrath, "Facing the Canon with Alister McGrath," Facing the Canon, November 28, 2014, YouTube video, 56:56, https://youtu.be/p3vVIBcpOBk.

3. Stephen C. Meyer, "Yes, Intelligent Design Is Detectable by Science," *Evolution News and Science Today*, April 24, 2018, https://evolutionnews.org/2018/04/yes-intelligent-design-is -detectable-by-science/.

4. Jonathan Witt, "Does George Smoot, Nobel Laureate, See Evidence of Design in the Cosmos?," *Evolution News and Science Today*, February 2, 2007, https://evolutionnews.org/2007/02 /does_george_smoot_nobel_laurea/.

5. Meyer, "Yes, Intelligent Design Is Detectable by Science."

6. *The Genius of Charles Darwin*, episode 2, "The Fifth Ape," directed by Russell Barnes, written by Richard Dawkins, aired August 11, 2008, on Channel 4.

7. Antony Flew with Roy Abraham Varghese, *There Is a God: How the World's Most Notorious Atheist Changed His Mind* (San Francisco: HarperOne, 2008), 80.

8. Dawkins, "The Fifth Ape."

9. Alister McGrath, "Augustine's Origin of Species," *Christianity Today*, May 2009, 40.

10. McGrath, "Augustine's Origin of Species," 39.

11. Sam Harris, "Best of Sam Harris Amazing Arguments and Clever Comebacks Part 4," Agatan Foundation, April 24, 2014, YouTube video, 19:41, https://youtu.be/nznnB9JAkVQ.

12. Dawkins, "The Fifth Ape."

13. Dawkins, "The Fifth Ape."

14. Flew with Varghese, *There Is a God*, 80.

15. McGrath, "Augustine's Origin of Species," 40.

16. McGrath, "Augustine's Origin of Species," 39.

Part 4: Introduction for Parents

1. N. T. Wright and Sean Kelly, "The Bible: Gospel, Guide, or Garbage?," December 12, 2013, in *Veritas Forum*, podcast, 1:32:04, http://www.veritas.org/the-bible-gospel-guide-or-garbage/.

2. "America's Changing Religious Landscape," Pew Research Center, May 12, 2015, https://www.pewforum.org/2015/05/12 /americas-changing-religious-landscape/.

3. Jürgen Habermas, *Time of Transitions* (Malden, MA: Polity, 2006), 151.

Chapter 10: The Church's Setup

1. N. T. Wright and Sean Kelly, "The Bible: Gospel, Guide, or Garbage?," December 12, 2013, in *Veritas Forum*, podcast, 1:32:04, http://www.veritas.org/the-bible-gospel-guide-or-garbage/.
2. Ryan Reeves, "Early Christian Persecution," Ryan Reeves, May 27, 2014, YouTube, 33:05, https://youtu.be/hJR0A9phBc8.
3. "Constantine," Christianity Today, accessed October 1, 2019, https://www.christianitytoday.com/history/people/rulers /constantine.html.
4. Reeves, "Early Christian Persecution."
5. "Constantine," Christianity Today.

Chapter 11: The Church's Breakups

1. Ryan Reeves, "Luther's Reformation (an Overview)," Ryan Reeves, January 21, 2016, YouTube video, 31:32, https://youtu .be/pX0oqGbSiG0.
2. Mark Hopkins, "What Did Spurgeon Believe?," *Christianity Today*, accessed October 1, 2019, https://www.christianitytoday .com/history/issues/issue-29/what-did-spurgeon-believe.html.
3. Ben Witherington III, "Ben Witherington III: The Problem with Evangelical Theology," Unitas Fidei, April 25, 2016, YouTube video, 31:29, https://youtu.be/ndJd1XFihe8.
4. Reeves, "Luther's Reformation."
5. Witherington, "The Problem with Evangelical Theology."
6. Kate Shellnutt, "Nobel Peace Prize Goes to Christian Doctor Who Heals Rape Victims," Christianity Today, October 5, 2018, https://www.christianitytoday.com/news/2018/october/denis -mukwege-congo-nobel-peace-prize.html.
7. Tracy Swartz, "Stephen Colbert Had a Life-Changing Experience in Chicago That Restored His Faith in God," *Chicago Tribune*, August 10, 2015, https://www.chicagotribune.com/entertainment /tv/ct-ent-stephen-colbert-catholic-late-show-20181119-story.html.

8. Shellnutt, "Nobel Peace Prize Goes to Christian Doctor."
9. Timothy Keller, "The Still Small Voice," Gospel in Life, September 26, 1999, 42:44, https://gospelinlife.com/downloads/the-still-small-voice-8969/.
10. Swartz, "Stephen Colbert Had a Life-Changing Experience."

Chapter 12: The Church's Future
1. Timothy J. Keller, "Sluggardliness," Gospel in Life, November 21, 2004, 40:05, https://gospelinlife.com/downloads/sluggardliness/.
2. Paul Vallely, "The Big Question: Was Cromwell a Revolutionary Hero or a Genocidal War Criminal?," *Independent*, September 4, 2008, http://www.independent.co.uk/news/uk/this-britain/the-big-question-was-cromwell-a-revolutionary-hero-or-a-genocidal-war-criminal-917996.html.
3. *New World Encyclopedia*, s.v. "Divine Right of Kings," last modified October 17, 2008, http://www.newworldencyclopedia.org/entry/Divine_Right_of_Kings.
4. "Know-Nothing Party," Ohio History Connection, accessed October 1, 2019, http://www.ohiohistorycentral.org/w/Know-Nothing_Party.
5. Gary Wolf, "The Church of the Non-Believers," *Wired*, November 1, 2006, https://www.wired.com/2006/11/atheism/.
6. Daniel Burke, "Millennials Leaving Church in Droves, Study Finds," CNN, May 14, 2015, https://www.cnn.com/2015/05/12/living/pew-religion-study/.
7. Wolf, "The Church of the Non-Believers." Emphasis in original.
8. Vallely, "The Big Question."
9. *New World Encyclopedia*, s.v. "Divine Right of Kings."
10. "Know-Nothing Party," Ohio History Connection.
11. Kathy Keller, "Flourishing Faith in Dangerous Places—Session 3—Kathy Keller," City to City Australia, July 29, 2014, 44:17, https://vimeo.com/101991490.
12. Timothy Keller, "Sluggardliness."
13. Lucette Verboven, "NT WRIGHT with Lucette Verboven,"

VodeoCatalog, accessed October 1, 2019, 25:57, https://vodeo
catalog.com/en/video/aoB10G3nm8o.
14. Ben Witherington III, "Ben Witherington III: The Problem
with Evangelical Theology," Unitas Fidei, April 25, 2016, You-
Tube video, 31:29, https://youtu.be/ndJd1XFihe8.
15. Witherington, "The Problem with Evangelical Theology."
16. Witherington, "The Problem with Evangelical Theology."
17. Ingrid Faro, "God's Comfort for Human Brokenness," in *Divine
Suffering: History, Theology, and Church*, ed. Andrew Schmut-
zer (Eugene, OR: Wipf & Stock, forthcoming).

Conclusion
1. Michael Halcomb and Ben Witherington III, "The Bible &
Science: Dr. Michael Halcomb & Dr. Ben Witherington III,"
tmichaelwhalcomb, YouTube, October 12, 2014, 51:58, https://
www.youtube.com/watch?v=tNv3ym57Qrs&t=52s.

Digging Deeper
1. For more on the Dead Sea Scrolls, see James VanderKam, *The
Dead Sea Scrolls Today*, rev. ed. (Grand Rapids: Eerdmans,
2012); Geza Vermes, *The Complete Dead Sea Scrolls in English*
(New York: Penguin, 2004); and Michael O. Wise, Martin G.
Abegg Jr., and E. Cook, *The Dead Sea Scrolls: A New Translation*
(San Francisco: HarperSanFrancisco, 2005), which contains an
English translation of 155 documents and fragments from the
Dead Sea Scrolls collection.
     DeadSeaScrolls.org hosts historical background to the dis-
covery of the scrolls with pictures of the caves and types of manuscripts found: https://www.deadseascrolls.org.il/learn-about
-the-scrolls/introduction?locale=en_US. The Digital Dead Sea
Scrolls project contains digital access to some of the major
scrolls with information about their discovery and significance:
http://dss.collections.imj.org.il. Ibiblio.org provides access to
the exhibit at the Library of Congress about the Dead Sea Scrolls,
including information about Qumran and links to other websites:

http://www.ibiblio.org/expo/deadsea.scrolls.exhibit/intro
.html. The Biblical Archaeology Society offers a free ebook
online with great information: https://www.biblicalarchaeology
.org/free-ebooks/the-dead-sea-scrolls-discovery-and-meaning/.
2. Flavius Josephus, *Josephus: The Essential Works*, ed. and trans.
   Paul L. Maier (Grand Rapids: Kregel Academic, 1994), 281–82.
3. For more examples of Jesus cited outside the Bible, see Darrell
   L. Bock, *Studying the Historical Jesus: A Guide to Sources and
   Methods* (Grand Rapids: Baker Academic, 2002); John P. Dickson, *A Doubter's Guide to Jesus: An Introduction to the Man from
   Nazareth for Believers and Skeptics* (Grand Rapids: Zondervan, 2018); Craig S. Keener, *The Historical Jesus of the Gospels*
   (Grand Rapids: Eerdmans, 2012); Christopher Klein, "The
   Bible Says Jesus Was Real. What Other Proof Exists?" History,
   April 16, 2019, https://www.history.com/news/was-jesus-real
   -historical-evidence; and Lawrence J. Mykytiuk, "Who Was
   Jesus: Exploring the History of Jesus' Life." Biblical Archaeology
   Society, 2015, https://www.biblicalarchaeology.org/free-ebooks
   /who-was-jesus-exploring-the-history-of-jesus-life/.
4. For more on Bible genres, look at these additional resources:
   Robert B. Chisholm Jr., *From Exegesis to Exposition: A Practical Guide to Using Biblical Hebrew* (Grand Rapids: Baker, 1999);
   Gordon D. Fee and Douglas Stuart, *How to Read the Bible for
   All Its Worth*, 4th ed. (Grand Rapids: Zondervan, 2014); Gordon D. Fee and Douglas Stuart, *How to Read the Bible Book by
   Book* (Grand Rapids: Zondervan, 2014); and E. Randolph Richards and Brandon J. O'Brien, *Misreading Scripture with Western
   Eyes: Removing Cultural Blinders to Better Understand the Bible*
   (Downers Grove, IL: InterVarsity, 2012).